A STUDENT'S GUIDE TO MONEY MATTERS

Your Financial Future Begins Now

Jacqueline S. Hodes, Ed.D. and Mary-Alice Ozechoski, M.A.

cognella® | ACADEMIC PUBLISHING

Bassim Hamadeh, CEO and Publisher
Kassie Graves, Acquisitions Editor
Berenice Quirino, Associate Production Editor
Miguel Macias, Senior Graphic Designer
Alexa Lucido, Licensing Associate
Don Kesner, Interior Designer
Natalie Piccotti, Senior Marketing Manager
Kassie Graves, Director of Acquisitions and Sales
Jamie Giganti, Senior Managing Editor

Printed in the United States of America

ISBN: 978-1-5165-3315-2 (pbk)

A STUDENT'S GUIDE TO MONEY MATTERS

Your Financial Future Begins Now

DEDICATION

We dedicate this book to all of our nieces, nephews, and god-
children who have or soon will navigate the path of figuring
out life after high school. We are proud of each of you!

THE COGNELLA SERIES ON STUDENT SUCCESS

Student success isn't always measured in straight As.

Many students arrive at college believing that if they study hard and earn top grades, their higher education experience will be a success. Few recognize that some of their greatest learning opportunities will take place outside the classroom. Learning how to manage stress, navigate new relationships, or put together a budget can be just as important as acing a pop quiz.

The Cognella Series on Student Success is a collection of books designed to help students develop the essential life and learning skills needed to support a happy, healthy, and productive higher education experience. Featuring topics suggested by students and books written by experts, the series offers research-based, yet practical advice to help any student navigate new challenges and succeed throughout their college experience.

Series Editor: Richard Parsons, Ph.D.
Professor of Counselor Education, West Chester University

Other titles available in the series:

- *A Student's Guide to Stress Management*
- *A Student's Guide to a Meaningful Career*
- *A Student's Guide to College Transition*
- *A Student's Guide to Self-Care*
- *A Student's Guide to Communication and Self-Presentation*
- *A Student's Guide to Exercise for Improving Health*

ABOUT THE AUTHORS

Y ou've probably heard that college is expensive and financing your education can be complex. While there's a lot of information available about financial aid, student loans, creating a college friendly budget, and more, it can be increasingly difficult to convert all that information into a financial plan that truly works for you.

A Student's Guide to Money Matters: Your Financial Future Begins Now will help you learn how to successfully finance your college education. The guide assists you in developing a full financial plan, so you can think critically about the costs of college, better assess what you truly can and can't afford, and make sound decisions that will ensure your financial health throughout your academic career.

Informative, accessible, and full of real-world examples, this guide will help you develop the financial savvy necessary to navigate the costs associated with investing in your education.

A Student's Guide to Money Matters is part of the Cognella Series on Student Success, a collection of books designed to help students develop the essential life and learning skills needed to support a happy, healthy, and productive higher education experience.

Jacqueline S. Hodes is an associate professor of higher education policy and student affairs at West Chester University. She earned a master's degree in education, with an emphasis in college counseling and student personnel services, and her doctoral degree in education, with an emphasis in educational leadership and higher education administration, from the University of Delaware.

Mary-Alice Ozechoski is the vice president of student affairs and traditional enrollment at Cedar Crest College. She earned her bachelor's degree in communications from Clarion University and her master's degree in counseling and student personnel services from Edinboro University.

CONTENTS

Unit I: Planning on Paying for College

Unit II: The Business of College

Unit III: Finances and Your Future

EDITOR'S PREFACE

T he transition to college marks a significant milestone in a person's life. Many of you will be preparing to live away from your friends and family for the very first time. Clearly this is and should be an exciting time.

It is a time to experience new things and experiment with new options. While the opportunity to grow is clear, so too are the many challenges you are to experience as you transition from high school to college.

Research suggests that the first year of college is the most difficult period of adjustment a student faces. Not only will you be required to adjust to new academic demands but you will also have to navigate a number of social and emotional challenges that accompany your life as a college student. The books found within this series—*Cognella Series on Student Success*—have been developed to help you with the many issues confronting your successful transition from life as a high school student to life as a collegiate. Each book within the series was designed to provide research-based, yet practical advice to assist you succeeding in your college experience.

While it may be obvious that developing your academic and social skills is essential to your successful college experience, it is also important to note that your ability to manage the stress associated with the entire college experience is equally essential to success. One specific contributor to the stress of the college experience is the need to navigate the complex process associated with financing a college education as well as managing one's finances while in college.

The current book, *A Student's Guide to Money Matters: Your Financial Future Begins Now* provides the reader with research-based practices for managing finances and making financial decisions as they relate to the funding of a college (and post-college) education. The book provides practical suggestions and advice for money management and engages the reader by way of numerous exercises and assessments. Written in a very engaging and reader-friendly manner, *A Student's Guide to Money Matters: Your Financial Future Begins Now* employs case illustrations in a feature called "*Voices From Campus,*" and opportunities to apply what you are learning in a feature called "*Your Turn.*"

I believe you will find this book to be a valuable guide to addressing the financial pressures you will encounter from the time of your college application and admission through to your preparation to enter life following graduation.

Richard Parsons, Ph.D.
Series Editor

AUTHORS' PREFACE

Y ou probably have heard that college is expensive. You may have heard your parents, family members, teachers, and friends talk about the high cost of college tuition and fees. The conversations are happening all around you—on the news, on social media, and at your kitchen table. College is expensive and the "price tag" will seem overwhelming to most students. We know you are already wondering how you and your family will afford this next step in your education.

Financing your college education can be complicated. You will have to make a lot of decisions in the next year or so. Many of those decisions will involve discussions about what you can and cannot afford. Sometimes students and families look at the total cost to attend a particular college or university and immediately remove it from consideration because it is too expensive. There are many steps to take before you make a decision about what you can afford. Talking about money and finances can be stressful, especially when you are embarking on a new experience!

In the chapters that follow you will learn about how to finance your college education. As you read through the book, you will begin to understand the many processes involved in developing a financial plan. The exercises included in the book will help you to think more deeply about the costs of college and assist you in making decisions about what is best for you. Included in each chapter are "voices" of students who are also learning about the cost of a college education. One student, Xander, is featured throughout the book. You can follow him as he learns about how to navigate the financing of a college degree.

Disclaimer: Both authors have over 30 years of experience in higher education. The information presented in this book represents their collective knowledge and advice about financing a college education. For specific information about your family's finances please consult with an accountant or the college/university office of financial aid.

JSH/MAO

ACKNOWLEDGMENTS

The authors wish to acknowledge Valerie Kreiser for the thoughtful review of this book. Her professional expertise as a financial aid administrator helped us to provide you the most current and accurate information. We also want to acknowledge Katie Myers for her work on preparing the many resources (In Print, On the Web, On Campus, and In the Community) in the appendix. As a current college student, she brought a sensitivity to the work and chose resources that will be most helpful to you, her peers.

UNIT I: PLANNING ON PAYING FOR COLLEGE

CHAPTER 1

UNDERSTANDING YOUR BUDGET: THE REAL COST OF COLLEGE

C ongratulations! It is that time. Time to decide about your life following your high school graduation. You may have always known that you wanted to attend college or maybe you recently decided that going to college is the next step in your education.

Regardless of what you know or hear from others, college is expensive. And it is also a good investment to make. As a young adult you are probably looking at the total cost for attending college and wondering how you will be able to pay for the education you desire. It is possible to figure it out but it will take some knowledge, research, thought, and creativity.

Lindsey

For my whole life, all I have wanted to do is to be a teacher. I know I must go to college to get my degree. I didn't really think about college until now. I am a high school junior and it seems that all anyone is talking about these days is which colleges they are visiting and want to attend. I am not sure which college I want to attend, but I know for sure that it has to be close to home, not more than two hours away. I want to live on campus and I also want to join a sorority.

I am so nervous about the cost of college. I've heard from my family and friends that college is so expensive. When alumni came to talk with us about going to college, they told us that they were going to graduate with a lot of debt. Debt, it scares me. When I started looking at college websites, I was confused. They all are different and the costs seem so complicated.

My parents just got a divorce and money is very tight. My mother is working two jobs and I am working in a day-care center after school. It is great experience, but I don't think I can make enough money to afford to go to college. I don't even know where to start!

You may have similar concerns as Lindsey. This book will help you to understand how to afford your education—one step at a time! At the end of this chapter you will find a worksheet (Worksheet 1.1: Cost of Attendance) which will help you to understand the total cost of attendance before financial aid is awarded.

1.1: Sticker Shock

As you begin to think about attending college, it is easy to be overwhelmed. There are so many questions swirling around in your head. Questions about majors, careers, admission requirements, type and location of college, friends, classes, and opportunities fill your thoughts. One very important question you must answer is, "How do I pay for all of this?"

When exploring colleges and universities, most students begin by looking on the college website. Once they locate the cost for attendance, they are typically surprised by the number … they experience what is called *sticker shock*. This number multiplied by four years can seem impossible to meet. Do not let this figure prevent you from exploring the wonderful opportunity for a college education. This book can help you trim that number to one that may be easier to manage.

So take a breath. And take another one. Now let us begin the process of understanding the real cost of college and how you can fund your dreams.

1.2: What's Your Type?

You have heard the expression, "Different strokes for different folks," right? This is so true when thinking about college choice. There are many different types of colleges and universities. It is important to think about what type of institution would be the best academic, social, and FINANCIAL match for you. Below is a description of the different types of higher education institutions.

Public/State Four-Year Colleges and Universities

Public or state colleges and universities are supported in part by the state in which they are located. The tuition cost for a student who has residence in the state (in-state) is lower than the tuition cost for a student who does not live in the state (out-of-state). In-state tuition is lower because students' families are paying state taxes which support their state colleges and universities. The cost for room, board, and fees remains the same for both in-state and out-of-state students. Public or state supported colleges and universities are often mid-size to large institutions and offer a wide variety of majors, degrees, and co-curricular opportunities.

Private Four-Year Colleges and Universities

Private colleges and universities are supported by your tuition dollars. Like public and state institutions, the cost for attendance is broken down into components including tuition, room, board, and fees. Therefore, the tuition cost for a private university is the same for in-state and out-of-state students. Private colleges and universities range in size, but many institutions are small to mid-sized. Some students know that they will be more successful in a small college environment, many of which are privately controlled.

Community Colleges (Two-Year)

Community colleges are often a first choice for students. The cost for attendance at a community college is broken down by tuition and fees. Some community colleges do provide housing. Housing costs would be above and beyond the cost of tuition. Community colleges are funded by the state and community in which they reside. Tuition costs will differ based on where you live. If you live in the community that helps to fund the college, your tuition will be lower than if you live outside of that community or outside the state. Like public or state colleges and universities, the fees are the same regardless of your residency.

Other Types of Colleges and Universities

There are many other types of colleges and universities for you to explore. You may be interested in a military career and might explore admission to the Army, Navy, or Air Force Academy. You may want to have a technical career in culinary arts or auto mechanics and look at for-profit or proprietary institutions. Regardless of the institution, there will be some costs associated with attendance.

1.3: Steps to Understanding the Bottom Line: Deconstructing the Cost

What Is Included in Tuition?

The first cost to consider is the cost for your classes. This cost is referred to as tuition. As explained above, sometimes the word tuition includes all the costs of attending college. In most cases, the tuition is the cost per credit.

The cost per credit will differ in a public/state college or university depending on your residency. The good news is that if you plan to attend as a full-time student (typically 12–15 credits per semester) the tuition will often be a flat fee and not a per credit cost. The even better news is that at many institutions, your flat fee tuition can include up to 18 credits! You will need to consult your college or university for their policies. For some motivated students, this is a real bargain. CAUTION: 15–16 credits is a very typical load for students, especially first-time, first-year students. Taking on additional credits may be a financial win, but it does not always pay off in the end if you cannot manage the workload. If you go over the 18 credits, there may be an additional cost per credit.

What Is Included in "Room"?

For many students, the college experience includes living on campus in a residence hall or other type of dwelling. On-campus residence is often referred to as "room." There are a wide variety of choices of residence hall living for students, depending on the size of the institution. There is a difference in cost depending on size, occupancy (how many students in each room), and amenities.

At many colleges and universities, there are "freshmen" residence halls where all first-year, first-time students are housed. At other schools, you may be able to choose your residence hall or you may be placed in a hall based on availability. There are many types of "rooms" on campus. Different types of housing include:

- Double Occupancy Rooms (two people sharing a room)
- Single Occupancy Rooms (one person living alone in a room)
- Suites (2–6+ people with common living space and bedrooms that may be single or double occupancy)
- Medical Single Rooms (one person living alone with a documented need)
- Apartments (a wide variety of occupancies and floor plans)

- Special Interest Housing (sometimes based on major, learning community, or co-curricular involvement; can also be based on a shared culture or faith)

Please see Your Turn 1.1 for questions to answer to help determine your residence hall needs and wants. Sometimes you are not able to choose but if you are, these answers will help guide your choice.

YOUR TURN 1.1

Where Should I Live?

Directions: Most often first-year students are housed in a double room with another student. You may not have a choice! Regardless, you may want to ask yourself these questions so you know your living style. Reflect on each main question and the follow-up information/questions. You may want to write down the answers or talk them through with trusted family members or friends. The answers to these questions will help you make decisions about living arrangements throughout your time in college.

1. What can you afford?
   - This is the first and most important question as finances will often determine your decision.
2. Have you had experience in sharing a room?
   - What was positive about the experience?
   - What was challenging about the experience?
3. Do you have any medical conditions that might dictate a particular living arrangement?
   - You will need to obtain documentation to obtain a "medical single."
4. Are you an introvert or an extrovert?
   - You may want to consider balancing your style with someone similar or different from you. There are pros and cons to both decisions.
5. Do you think you will use your room for sleeping? Studying? Socializing?

- Do you want your room to be a place for "hanging out" or your private sanctuary?

6. Are your major classes in one location on campus?

- What is the closest residence hall to where the majority of your classes are held?

7. Are you open to sharing your belongings?

- Shared space often means sharing a television, refrigerator, and a bathroom.

8. Would you be comfortable sharing living spaces with people who have shared interests or experiences?

- Many colleges offer learning community housing both in residence halls and on-campus houses. These living opportunities will connect you with students who share your interests.

What Is Included in "Board"?

Typically, if you live on campus in a campus residence hall you will be obligated to purchase a meal plan. A meal plan is often referred to as "board." Like residence hall options, meal plan options vary from campus to campus. You will want to weigh the various meal plan options to figure out which one matches your lifestyle and budget. Typical meal plans are listed below:

- Unlimited dining (typically the most expensive)

  You can go in and out of the dining hall all day long and eat as much as you want.

- 19 meals per week.

  Most typical meal plan. Includes three meals per day (Monday–Friday) and two meals per day on the weekends.

- Block meal plan.

  Allows you a set number of meals per semester.

- Flexible spending plan.

Allows for a fixed number of meals per week and additional dollars for other retail dining operations on campus.

- Often the above plans come with additional flexible (flex) dollars.

Please see Your Turn 1.2 for questions to help determine your meal plan needs and wants. Again, like residence halls, you may have limited choices of plans based on the individual campus offerings and requirements. Most campuses require students who are living on campus to have one of the larger meal plans. Tip: During your first year, you may want to track how many meals you actually use so you can make a good decision in following years.

YOUR TURN 1.2

I Am Hungry!

Directions: Choosing the best meal plan can be confusing. It will be hard to know what your schedule and eating habits will be during the semester. Most campuses require a meal plan for all first-year students living on campus, so you may not have a lot of options. Reflect on each question and the information below each question. You may want to write down the answers or talk them through with trusted family members or friends. The answers to these questions will help you make decisions about which meal plan to purchase.

1. Ideally, do you typically eat three meals a day?
   - If you like to eat breakfast, lunch, and dinner, then the full board plan (unlimited or 19 meals) may be the best option for you! It will allow you to eat each meal in the dining hall with no additional expense.

2. What is your schedule?
   - If your schedule does not start until late morning and you know you are a late sleeper, you may decide to get a reduced plan that does not include breakfast. Breakfast is an important meal so you may need to supply your own breakfast food.

- If your classes are back-to-back and you are in class during the meal time, you may want a reduced plan. Please note: Many dining services will pack a meal for you to pick up earlier in the day.

3. Do you have any dietary restrictions?

- Many dining services can accommodate dietary restrictions so please make sure to ask before deciding. If you have a dietary restriction that cannot be accommodated and you have documentation (typically from a physician or religious leader), you may be able to get a meal plan waiver. In this case, you will be financially responsible for providing your own meals.

4. What can you afford?

- If you are living on campus, you will most likely be required to purchase a meal plan. You can opt for a less expensive meal plan and purchase food to prepare on your own.

What Is Included in "Fees"?

If you are attending a public or state college or university, you may continue to be surprised about the cost when you look at the fees. Often the housing, meal, and other fees are equal or more than the cost of tuition. At private institutions, many fees are typically included in the total cost of attendance. Fees vary from institution to institution. Listed below are the typical fees and a short description of each. Most fees are mandatory. If you can opt out of the fee, the institution will indicate that option and what parameters must be met to eliminate the fee.

1. Educational Services Fee

Many schools have a "catch all" fee that pays for a variety of services on campus. For example, the general fee might include instructional equipment and supplies, library circulation materials, funding for other services such as tutoring and supplemental instruction. In most cases, the fee will cover the use of these services, although occasionally additional small fees are assessed per use.

2. Course/Class Fees

Many courses/classes require additional resources. You may be additionally charged for courses/classes that rely on these instructional resources. Examples include lab fees, clinical fees, art studio fees, distance learning fees, etc.

3. Student Activities Fee

As a typical college student you will spend the majority of your time outside of the classroom. This time is spent studying, working, volunteering, and also having fun! The out-of-classroom experiences such as student activities and programs, athletics, and clubs and organizations are funded through this fee. This fee allows colleges and universities to offer many free or reduced cost activities such as current movies, film series, guest lectures, concerts, comedians, road trips to cities and sporting events, intramurals, and traditional campus events such as family weekends and Homecoming. The activities fee is your ticket to fun, social experiences across campus!

4. Technology/Communication Fee

Technology and communication fees pay for computing services, campus Wi-Fi, computer labs, computer printing (either a weekly or semester page limit), cable access, etc. This fee helps institutions keep pace with the ever-changing world of technology.

5. Health Center/Student Health Insurance Fee

You want to stay healthy as a college student! The health center fee typically includes general health and wellness services. The services will vary by institution. Some colleges and universities provide simple medical exams whereas others provide comprehensive services including preventative care. Some health centers also charge a co-pay for visits and for prescriptions.

Colleges and universities may charge you for student health insurance on your bill. If you are covered by a parent or guardian, you can most likely waive this fee by providing documentation of your coverage. You will want to consult with the college or university to ensure that your plan will be sufficient, especially if you are traveling out of state.

6. Orientation Fee

As a college student, you will want to start off on the "right foot" and orientation is a great way to begin your college experience. Orientation typically takes place during the summer or right before the start of the fall or spring semester. Attendance at Orientation is often mandatory. There is typically a fee for attending. Parents and families are often invited to Orientation and there may be a separate fee for them to attend.

7. Parking and Building Fees

During your time in college you will most likely see construction on your campus. College and university buildings and parking lots need to be repaired and restored. New facilities may be constructed and existing facilities renovated or expanded. At public and state institutions, the cost of these repairs and construction are shared by the students. These fees will be discussed at student government meetings and voted on by the student body.

At some institutions, you may be able to have your vehicle. To park your car on campus you will need to purchase a parking permit. Parking permit costs differ from institution to institution and range from no cost to several hundred dollars a semester. You will want to explore these costs and policies before bringing your car to campus. Not purchasing a parking permit and illegally parking will result in a multitude of tickets and parking fines! Fines are placed on your student account, and unpaid fines can result in blocking your ability to register for classes or select a room for the following year. Each campus will have specific consequences for unpaid fines.

8. Identification (ID) Card Fee

A college ID card is important for many reasons. The ID card is used in the dining halls, the library, and to gain access to buildings, specifically your residence hall if you are living on campus. You may also need your ID card to gain entrance to athletic events and computer labs. When you are off campus, your ID card is proof that you are a student and often allows you to obtain a discount on certain services such as movies, museums, and restaurants. There is typically a charge to obtain your initial ID card and an additional charge to replace it if lost or stolen!

9. Payment Plan Fee

Many institutions will allow you to pay your bill in installments, but there is a fee for doing so. Pay special attention to your bill so you know if there is a charge for choosing the payment plan! Typically, it is a small fee but it adds to the total cost.

What Are "Miscellaneous Costs"?

Unlike most students' high school experiences, the cost for higher education is far from "all-inclusive." As you can see from the information above, there are many costs that are required for enrollment. You are probably thinking that there could not be any additional costs possible. Think again! Listed below are descriptions of costs that students often do not consider as they make their college financial plan.

1. Transportation

Even if you are living on campus and not commuting from home or an off-campus location, you will need to consider transportation costs. You need to think about the cost to get back and forth from home to school at the beginning and end of the school year as well as school breaks and holidays. If you select an institution that is far from your home and you plan to visit your family during breaks, you may need to factor in the cost of plane/train/bus fares. If your college or university is a large institution, there will most likely be a campus bus system for local travel. If you are in the city, you can take advantage of the public transportation system. But if you are in a more suburban or rural location, you will need to consider transportation costs (your own vehicle, car service, cab, etc.). Students who commute from home or live off campus should factor in the cost of gas, parking, tolls, and vehicle maintenance. It is important to remember to budget for these expenses.

2. Books

You probably already know that college textbooks are expensive, but you will most likely be surprised by the cost of just one semester of textbooks. Depending on your course of study, the cost of books may be reasonable. Or you may be shocked to know that one book can cost several hundred dollars!

There are several options to obtain your books. You can purchase a brand-new textbook or a used textbook from your campus store or an online store. When you purchase your textbooks, you can try to sell them back (for a reduced cost) at the end of the semester. Some students choose to rent their textbooks for a smaller cost. You must be VERY careful to note the return dates for textbook rentals as late charges can obliterate the savings from renting. You also want to make sure to read the rental agreement carefully as there may be rules about what you can (and cannot) do with the book (e.g., highlight). You can share a book with a friend or classmate but you run the risk of not having access to the book when you need it to study for a test. Finally, faculty will often put a copy of the textbook on reserve at the college/university library. The reserve copies are kept in a special room. You can use the book in the library only and only when another student is not using it!

3. Supplies

You will need basic school supplies depending on how you like to take notes in your classes. You will need notebooks, pens, etc. Depending on your major, there may be very specific supplies required such as a scientific calculator, lab coat, stethoscope, art supplies, and instruments to name a few. Most students come to college with a mobile device and have budgeted for this expense. Although campuses have computer labs for student use, most students benefit from having their own personal computer. Your campus information technology department will often have recommendations for the most appropriate type of technology to consider to help you be successful.

If you are living on campus, you will need to purchase all the supplies you want to make your residence hall room feel like home. Please see the following list of basic items. Most major retailers have a more comprehensive list on their websites.

Basic Campus Residence Hall Checklist

- ✔ Bed pillows
- ✔ Mattress pad
- ✔ Sheets
- ✔ Comforter/blanket
- ✔ Towels

✔ Shower caddy/shoes

✔ Personal care and grooming Items

✔ Kitchen tools (plates, forks, etc.)

✔ Hangers

✔ Umbrella

✔ Laundry basket/detergent

✔ Fan

✔ Desk lamp

✔ School supplies

✔ Surge protector/extension cords

✔ Decorations

4. Laundry

Some of you may have never done laundry for yourself. You may decide to wait until you can go home to get it done, but this is usually not the best solution for most students. Most students living on campus will need to do laundry at some point. Some institutions offer free washers and dryers in the residence hall. Many do not! You may be able to pay for the washer and dryer using your ID card or you may need to insert real money. You will also need to consider the cost of laundry supplies (i.e., detergent, etc.).

5. Food and Entertainment

College students get hungry ... and not just for breakfast, lunch, and dinner. Your meal plan typically covers your meals when you eat in the dining hall or other food venues on campus. But when you are cramming for a test at 2:00 in the morning, you may want to have a pizza delivered. These late-night take-out orders can add up!

As discussed above, your student activities fee covers many of the programs and services on campus. Depending on where your campus is located, you will want to take advantage of cultural events, sporting events, and other types of entertainment in the region. These experiences all cost money. Remember though, your ID card might get you a student discount!!

1.4: Can I Get Any of This on Sale?

At this point you are probably still wondering if you can afford these costs. Understandable. A college education is expensive but there are ways to make it more affordable. The next chapter will walk you through the financial aid process and how to obtain financial assistance to attend college. Below are two factors that are not immediately known to many families and can reduce the cost of attendance.

"Discount" Rates

Many colleges and universities offer merit scholarships in the acceptance letter. These are not funds the institution is giving to you. Rather, they are discounting their stated tuition dollars by offering you a scholarship based on your high school grade point average (GPA), involvement, and SAT/ACT scores. These scholarships are renewable year over year (up to a maximum of four to five years) based on criteria that usually includes achieving a certain cumulative GPA. Once you are enrolled in the college/university, it is important to know the GPA requirement so you know what grades you need to achieve to maintain the "discount."

Scholarships

Scholarships are not "one size fits all." They come in all shapes and sizes. You are probably most familiar with academic scholarships and athletic scholarships. Schools offer both types of scholarships but they vary based on the institution's size and control (either public or private). Your college or university may offer you a one-year scholarship or a scholarship that is available for your entire academic career, based again on your academic performance. Many private schools also offer legacy scholarships to students who have parents who are alumni.

You may be able to apply for scholarships in your community through your local religious institution and non-profit community agencies (e.g., Boys and Girls Clubs). Scholarship opportunities may be available through your parents' workplace or union.

When applying for outside scholarships (not on your campus) you will need to remember the following:

- Use all the resources available to you to research as many opportunities as possible.
- Search the Internet using a variety of online resources listed at the end of this book.
- Look often. New scholarships can be posted and advertised every day.
- If a personal statement is required, make sure it is concise, well-written, and free of errors.
- Have a list of references with phone numbers and email addresses ready to go as you are applying for scholarships.
- Note and meet all deadlines!
- Apply only for scholarships where you are eligible. If the scholarship is for a student who has a parent who is a mail carrier or a military veteran and your parent does not meet that parameter, do not apply!
- Any opportunity where you meet the criteria, APPLY!

VOICES FROM CAMPUS 1.2

Xander

I have always known I was going to go to college. I can't remember a time that my parents and I were not talking about what would happen once I graduated from high school. I thought that getting into a really top-rated school was my number one concern. Now that I have really started researching colleges and my options, I am finding getting into college is only one piece of figuring this whole thing out. The cost of attending college, living on campus, and having money for all the expenses is going to play a bigger role in my decision than I imagined.

1.5: The Take Away

- College costs vary by institutional type. You will need to understand which type of college is the best match for you and for your budget.
- College is expensive. You will need to do research on the total cost of attendance for each college or university you are interested in attending.
- There are many "hidden" costs to attend college. It is important to consider them all as you prepare your budget.

Worksheet 1.1: Cost of Attendance

Directions: Insert the name of each college or university you wish to attend. Then, navigate to each website to locate the information you need to understand the cost of attendance. You may need to estimate the cost of some expenses based on your specific situation.

	Institution A	Institution B	Institution C	Institution D	Institution E	Institution F	Institution G	Institution H
Cost of Attendance								
Base Tuition								
Housing Cost								
Meal Plan Cost								
Educational Services Fee								
Course/Class Fee								
Student Activities Fee								
Technology & Communication Fee								
Health Center/Health Insurance Fee								
Orientation Fee								
Parking & Building Fees								
ID Card Fee								
Payment Plan Fee								
Estimated Cost of Books								
Transportation Cost								
Other Fees								
Pre-Financial Aid Cost								

CHAPTER 2

FORMS, FILING, AND FINANCES

Now that you have some understanding of what you need to consider as you review your higher education options, it is time to begin the process of figuring out how to finance your dreams. A few very fortunate students do not need to read this chapter. But if you are like 85 percent of the American students (National Center for Education Statistics) wishing to pursue higher education, you will need to pay close attention to the information about forms and filing deadlines.

Colette

I am a senior in high school and I know it is supposed to be the best year of my life. It is, for the most part. Senior year is filled with so many wonderful moments that are going to be memories for a lifetime. But always in the back of my mind I am thinking about college and what next year might bring for me. I have been accepted at a few schools so far and I am so excited to know that I have somewhere to go. I am really waiting to hear from my very first-choice college, and I should hear any day.

My parents and I are planning to figure out just how much it will cost to attend the schools I have already heard from this month. I know they are worried about the costs. My first-choice school is much more expensive than my other choices. I overheard my parents talking about how nervous they are to fill out the paperwork. I am the first one in my family to go to college so I understand that they don't have all the answers. It seems so confusing and complex. Where do I start?

2.1: Focus Is Key

Talking about money and finances can cause a lot of stress and anxiety. A college education is expensive; in fact, it may be one of the largest expenses you ever have in your life. Completing financial aid forms can be a headache and feel like a chore. Yet, it is very important to complete these forms as soon as possible so you can understand your financial aid award. Once you understand your award and how much money you have available, you are one step closer to making your college choice.

Financing your education is complicated. The process can be overwhelming, even for those who have a lot of knowledge about finances. So take a breath. And take another one! Read through this chapter before you get started.

2.2: What Is Financial Aid?

Financial aid is an often-misunderstood term. Financial aid comes to the student in various forms. Some aid is given to the student as a grant or a scholarship that does not need to be repaid. Other aid gives the student (or parents/guardian) access to take out low-interest loans. Some aid allows students to earn money while working on campus. Financial aid often comes from the federal or state government but can also be accessed through the college/university, banks, private foundations and donors, religious organizations, and community agencies.

Federal financial aid is accessed through completing the Free Application for Federal Student Aid (FAFSA) form. You cannot obtain federal financial aid without completing this form. Grants, loans, and work-study jobs are types of federal financial aid. State funds are also available to eligible students. These funds are often given to the student as grants or access to low-interest loans. You can find out more information about your state's policies and procedures at www.studentaid.ed.gov.

Federal and state financial aid may not provide you with enough funds to finance your degree. The allocated funds are based on many factors, including your family income and expenses. Most students find they have a financial gap between their aid and the cost of attendance. To close the gap, you will need to explore and take advantage of other available opportunities to receive additional financial assistance. These opportunities are discussed later in the chapter. Most funding agencies and entities use information from your FAFSA to, in part, make decisions about aid for you. Let us begin with instructions for filling out this essential document.

2.3: The FAFSA

There are many forms to complete as you begin to finance your education. Typically, your high school counseling office (guidance office) will have information about many of the forms you need. The FAFSA is the most important form and the first one to complete. You will have to complete this form each year you attend college (more on this later in Chapters 4 and 5). This is a government form that can be found at https://fafsa.ed.gov/. It is important to review this form and all others carefully. Pay attention to all the details! A small error or a missing field can delay the processing of your form and your financial aid award.

Below are your first initial steps:

1. Make sure you have all the necessary basic information required.

   a. If you have filed taxes, you will need your tax returns. Make sure you are using the correct year of your tax return!

   b. Most students are dependents of their parents or a guardian. You will need their tax returns to complete the FAFSA.

   c. If you have a checking or savings account, you will need access to that information. And you will need your parents' or guardian's bank information.

   d. You need your social security number and your parents' or guardian's social security numbers too!

   e. If you have a driver's license, you will need to provide your license number.

   f. If you are not a U.S. citizen, you will need to provide your alien registration number.

   g. Some students and families have more complex financial situations so you should check the FAFSA website for additional requirements for filing.

2. Set aside enough time to complete the forms in one sitting. You may need to carve out at least two to three hours of uninterrupted time. You might not use all that time but you will be glad to have it available if you run into complications. Starting and stopping midway through this process will not be in your best interest.

3. Choose a place to work where you have access to a table and the Internet. Some families may want to sit at their kitchen or dining room table, others may find it easier to go to the public library. Regardless of where you work, you want to be able to have room for all the paperwork.

4. Get organized. We each have an organizational system that works for us. You may like to use sticky notes to mark places to sign or a calendar to write down individual deadlines. You may want to have a folder for all your forms or a separate folder for each form. Regardless, you need a system to keep track of the information. You will want to record usernames, passwords, and PINs. When you

complete a form online, you will want to print out a copy and the confirmation that it was submitted. Do what works best for you but do something!

5. Pay attention to filing dates for your state. Each state has a different deadline to submit the FAFSA. These dates are listed on the FAFSA website.

2.4: Ready, Set, FILE!

Now that you are organized and have all your documents available follow the steps below to file your FAFSA.

1. **Access the FAFSA form at https://fafsa.ed.gov/**. Make sure you use this website as it is FREE! There are other websites where you pay a fee to complete the information and they send it to FAFSA. This is not necessary.

2. **Create your FSA ID at https://fsaid.ed.gov/**. You will want to create an FSA ID for many reasons. The FSA ID allows you access your FAFSA application, make changes easily, and electronically sign documents. Both the student and the parents/guardian need to create the FSA ID to legally sign all government and other documents. To create an FSA ID you need to choose a username and password. Save this information in a safe place!

3. **Complete the form**. This sounds simple. The FAFSA is a user-friendly form that has instructions at each stage. Make sure you read each question carefully before answering. The online form has many opportunities for help if you need it.

4. **Hit SUBMIT!** But don't forget to sign with your FSA ID for you and your parents/guardian before you submit. Once you submit your form it will be routed to your selected colleges and universities, your home state higher education agency, and the state agencies where your selected schools are located. Submitting your information electronically allows for a quick and efficient process. If your information changes over time, you can access your FAFSA account using your

FSA ID and make the corrections or updates. NOTE: If you make any corrections, you and your parents/guardian will need to sign the FAFSA again.

5. **Monitor your email for your Student Aid Report (SAR).** It should be sent to you within three weeks. You need to review this report to make sure it is error free. You may want to have your parents/guardian look it over too! If you did make a mistake, you can correct it by going back into your FAFSA account online. Remember, if you are unsure whether you need to make changes to your FAFSA, make sure to contact the financial aid office at the college or university.

6. **Now you need to wait!** Each college or university where you have been admitted will send you a financial aid award letter. Patience is key as each institution has its own timeline for sending out this information.

2.5: Making Sense of Your Financial Aid Award

Congratulations! You now have your financial aid award letters from your chosen institutions. Now it is time to make sense of each individual award and what it will mean as you make your enrollment decision. Keep in mind that you are free to accept or reject any or all the aid you are offered. And remember that the financial aid award is for both the fall and spring semesters. Below is a description of what you may see listed in your award letter:

- **College/University Scholarships**. You may receive scholarships from the college/university due to your academic achievements, special abilities, or talents. The good news is that this aid does not need to be repaid. The amount of scholarship dollars you are receiving will be broken out for two semesters. The letter will indicate if the scholarship(s) is renewable and the terms (e.g., minimum grade point average, earned credits) needed to renew it each year of enrollment.

- **Grants**. Grants are also a form of financial aid that does not have to be repaid. There are many types of grants. Some may be awarded from the federal government. State governments also award grants. Private institutions may award grants as well. Again, the funds are split over two semesters and may or may not be available in the following year. The award is based on your current FAFSA information.

- **Loans**. Loans in your award letter are made to you from the federal government and come in two forms: *Federal Direct Subsidized* loans and *Federal Direct Unsubsidized* loans. Federal Direct Subsidized loans allow you to borrow money that must be repaid when you graduate or leave higher education. The good news about Federal Direct Subsidized loans is that the interest is paid by the federal government while you are enrolled in school. The downside of taking Federal Direct Unsubsidized loans is that you must pay the interest on your own when the loan is disbursed to the school. You can defer the interest, but it will continue to accrue and be added to your balance upon graduation or when you leave higher education. Remember, there are limits to the amount of funds you can borrow.

- **Federal Work-Study**. Your award letter might indicate that you have been given a work-study position. A work-study job allows you to earn money by working on or off campus at an approved job site. Often these jobs are in university offices, the dining hall, community service agencies, or other local non-profit organizations in the college or university community. The money allocated to you from the work-study program must be earned by you and you can decide how to apply those funds. You can put these funds towards your tuition and fees or you may use this money to offset your other personal expenses.

- **Federal Direct Plus Loan**. More good news! Your parents or guardians are also able to apply for a loan, also known as the Parent PLUS loan. Some colleges and universities list this information on the award letter; others do not. The Parent PLUS loan is taken out in your parents'/guardian's name and applied to your bill. The payments start once your loan is fully disbursed to the college. However, your parents/guardian can request a deferment on the Parent PLUS loan while you are enrolled in school (part time or full time). Your parents/guardian does not have to make payment while the loan is deferred. If your parents/guardian is denied the Parent PLUS loan, you may be eligible for additional unsubsidized loans.

Jamal

I am so excited to start college in the fall. I applied to my top-choice school and guess what? I GOT IN! I have been to campus twice this year and have met so many great people already. I am excited to live in the residence hall and get involved in student government. Tosh, my campus ambassador (tour guide), gave a great tour of campus. I saw classrooms, the gym, a residence hall room, and even had my picture taken with the mascot! I think I could be an ambassador once I get to campus. Tosh told me to apply in October if I am interested.

One thing is bothering me though…my financial aid award letter. I got a lot of financial aid, I even was awarded a work-study job but it is not enough to pay the bill. My parents are going to talk with my grandparents about helping me this first year, but I wish I knew where else I could go to get some money. I have a job now but it only pays minimum wage, and there is no way I can earn enough money before the bill is due. Help!

2.6: Closing the Gap: What If Your Award Is Not Enough?

Tuition and fees are as varied as the many higher education institutions. Many times, the financial aid award cannot meet the financial cost to attend the institution. You will want to have a family discussion to evaluate your options based on your interests, your financial aid award, and your available funds. There are other ways to explore closing the financial gap so you can pursue your dreams.

Private Loans

You and/or your parents/guardian can apply for a private loan from a bank or a credit union. These loans are not included in your original financial aid award and therefore have rules and regulations that are different than the Federal Direct Subsidized or Unsubsidized loans discussed earlier. The best advice is to visit your bank or credit union to discuss the terms of a private loan. You can also check your college/university website to see if they have a list of preferred lenders. The benefits include having funds to pay for your education. The liabilities may be the cost of the interest and the repayment schedule.

YOUR TURN 2.1

Where Can I Find Scholarships?

Directions: Many colleges and universities will offer you scholarship dollars as part of your financial aid package. You may need additional resources to cover the cost of your education. There are often other resources in your community that come from civic organizations, religious communities, and community agencies that provide scholarships to prospective and current college students. Keep in mind that each scholarship application will have unique requirements and deadlines. As you research these opportunities make sure to pay attention to these requirements and deadlines.

Below are some resources for you to review. If you check yes, follow the suggested next steps to explore what additional scholarship opportunities might be available for you.

1. Are you a member of a religious community or place of worship?

    ___Yes ___No

    • Contact the religious leader at your place of worship and inquire about scholarships available to members and the application process.

2. Are your parents or guardian members of a labor union?

    ___Yes ___No

- Look online at the labor union's website to determine if they award scholarships to members' college-bound dependents. If so, you will need to verify your parent or guardian's union membership when you apply for these awards.

3. Are you or your family members involved in a civic organization such as the local Chamber of Commerce, Kiwanis, or Rotary Club?

    ___Yes   ___No

- Contact the organization by phone or email and ask about funding. For these types of organizations, you should be prepared to include information about community service and leadership activities which you have participated in throughout high school.

4. Are you a Girl Scout?   ___Yes   ___No

- The Girl Scouts awards scholarships to members who have achieved silver or gold status in some regions. Check with your regional Girl Scouts office for details on applying for these funds.

5. Are you a Boy Scout?   ___Yes   ___No

- The Boy Scouts awards funds to young men who have achieved Eagle Scout status in some regions. Check with your regional Boy Scouts office for details on applying for these funds.

6. Are you currently employed at a part-time job?   ___Yes   ___No

- Ask the human resource department at your job if the company offers scholarships to employees. You may be eligible based on your hours of service to the company. Some companies require that when you are home for holidays and breaks that you return to the job or if you are commuting to a local college that you maintain your employment.

7. Are your parents or guardians employed?   ___Yes   ___No

- Your parent or guardian should contact the human resource department at their workplace to determine if their employer offers scholarships to dependents.

8. Are you a member of a club athletic team?   ___Yes   ___No

- Some club athletic programs offer scholarship awards to college-bound team members. Contact your coach to see if your team offers these types of awards.

9. Have you been a volunteer at a local non-profit organization?

___Yes ___No

- If you have been a long-term volunteer at a local hospital or non-profit organization, contact your supervisor to see if they offer scholarships to students.

This list is not exhaustive. You undoubtedly have unique and individual talents and strengths. If you are involved in an organized activity or have a special skill or talent, do some research about scholarship opportunities related to those activities or talents. You never know what might be available!

Scholarships not connected to your university are available to you if you are willing to spend time investigating and applying for them. The exercise below will help you begin your exploration by understanding your unique qualities and any activities that might make you eligible for certain scholarships. There are scholarships that are connected to your religious institution, service organizations, your parents'/guardian's employment, labor union, or their involvement in civic organizations. Popular scholarship search engines include www.myscholly.com and www.careeronestop.org. Please see the Appendix for more information on scholarships.

Each scholarship is unique and has varying features, rules, deadlines, and parameters. You will need to carefully read the information about each one as you are applying. The organizational system you set up earlier can help you keep track of your scholarship application process.

If you receive a scholarship from an outside source, it may or may not impact your financial aid award. As you receive scholarship notifications, you will want to inform your institutions' office of financial aid.

Part-Time Jobs

It is most likely that you had or currently have a part-time job. You may work 10–20 hours a week at a restaurant, retail store, or other venue. You may babysit or cut lawns. You may tutor or teach music lessons. You may work in the summer so you can focus on your schoolwork during the academic year. You may have a job that you can do online.

Having a part-time job while you are in college is one small way to supplement your finances and offset the cost of college. A part-time job during the school year will not significantly reduce the expenses, but it will help you with funds to pay for food, supplies, books, entertainment, and transportation. You may want to consider summer employment if you need to make a more significant financial impact on your "bottom line."

A part-time job will certainly provide you with funds and give you some insight into the world of work. Your part-time employment also gives you access to supervisors who may be able to serve as a reference for you as you apply for other positions, for scholarships, and/or for graduate school. You can explore both on-campus and off-campus employment. Both have benefits and challenges. In Chapter 6 you will learn a lot more about how to get a job on campus.

On-Campus Employment

As discussed above, a federal work-study position is often a part-time job on campus and connected to your financial aid package. There are other part-time positions on college campuses that are not classified as federal work-study. Depending on your institution's policy, you may be able to have a federal work-study position and a non-work-study position. The non-work-study positions may be listed on the institution's employment website or through the career development center. When you work on campus, you typically do not have any transportation concerns and you have a supervisor who understands the academic calendar. Unfortunately, most on-campus employment ceases during holiday breaks and summer, reducing your earning potential.

Again, please see Chapter 6 for a more detailed discussion of on-campus employment and for a listing of possible on-campus employment.

Off-Campus Employment

Regardless of your financial aid award, you may decide to pursue off-campus employment. These positions may be listed through your campus career development center. You can find off-campus employment in the same way you did in high school—filling out applications! You may also find employment such as babysitting or lawn care through networking with faculty and staff.

When you work off campus it is important to remember that you may have to get to and from your job. You must build in transportation time. It is also important to note that the busiest times for retail employment (Thanksgiving through January) are also the busiest times for college students (end of the semester and fall semester finals). You may be able to keep your job during the holiday breaks and you may be able to earn a higher hourly wage.

VOICES FROM CAMPUS 2.3

Xander

I visited my school counselor's office to ask for advice about financial aid. My counselor is really nice but it was like he was speaking a different language: FAFSA, subsidized loans, unsubsidized loans, Parent PLUS loans, selected for verification, all these new concepts! I am trying not to get overwhelmed, but I feel like I need an accountant to help me. I keep telling myself I can learn everything to make sure I get as much funding as possible. I hope I'm right!

2.7: The Take Away:

- Filing the FAFSA is important and is time sensitive. You want to make sure that you start the paperwork early. You can begin filing your FAFSA on October 1.

- Read your financial aid award carefully and contact the office of financial aid at the institution if you have questions.

- Knowing the costs of attendance and what you can afford will help in your decision making.

- When the financial aid award is not sufficient, do not panic. You can explore various means of "closing the gap."

NOW WHAT?: MAKING A COLLEGE COMMITMENT

O kay. You have your acceptance letters. You may have a rejection or two and you may have been wait-listed at an institution. You also have your financial aid award letter and more information on available and possible scholarships. You understand how much money you should earn before the start of school and whether you need a part-time job while in school. You have explored ways to close the financial gap, at least for this first year. Now you must make your decision about which college or university to attend. This is an exciting and daunting moment.

Zachary

It was pretty exciting opening the mail and my email and hearing back from the colleges and universities about whether I had been accepted. I admit, I didn't get into every place I applied and at one school I am on the wait-list. Now I also know what kind of financial aid I will receive from each school. This information makes my choice harder because now I know what the cost of attending will be ... and so do my parents.

I want to make a good decision about my education *and* my finances. My family and I are sitting down to look at each financial aid package and to talk about them. I'm nervous about the conversation because I've never really talked about money and these kinds of expenses with my parents. I know it is a big decision for everyone.

3.1: Weighing the Pros and Cons: A First Look

Many prospective college students have a "first choice" school. It may be your dream institution. When you visited the school, you could see yourself walking to and attending classes, studying for challenging exams, eating in the dining hall, and hanging out with new friends. As your acceptance letters arrive with your financial aid awards and you examine the cost and the award, you may have a hunch that your dream may not become a reality. Do not give up hope yet.

It is important to have all the information in one place so you can make an informed decision that fits your budget, your interests, and your desires. At the end of the chapter is a worksheet (Worksheet 3.1: Weighing the Costs) that you can use to help you determine the best financial and educational decision for you and your family.

For most students and families the first consideration is cost. You need to understand what you can reasonably afford, not just for this year but for every year as you complete your degree. This is a very important conversation to have with your family. There might be a lot of support and information as you plan for the first year of college and when you are done, you may think you do not have to think about it again. However, it is important to additionally plan for four or more years of expenses. It is also easy to believe that you will be in a better financial place when your loans come due. Remember your loans will come due just six months after graduation! If your family took out loans for you, they may be paying on them immediately. It behooves you to be VERY realistic about what you can afford.

Ideally, you did your research as you were applying to colleges, so you have a good understanding of the total cost of attendance for one year. You also completed your FAFSA and understand the funds you have available as you consider your choices. You can calculate the cost you still need to meet. You COULD make your decision just using this information, with the lowest cost institution being your choice. But wait! Although finances play a big part in your decision, there is more to consider as you weigh the pros and cons of attending each institution. You also must do a "reality" check. If the remaining costs are impossible to meet, you may want to eliminate that choice from your list. But wait again! You may want to read further in this chapter to see how you might be able to appeal your financial aid award.

Before you make your college or university choice based solely on finances, you want to consider a few other factors. One important concept to consider is the value proposition. You may not have a good understanding of what the value proposition entails. It is difficult to determine the value proposition for each institution because each individual student will have a unique collegiate experience. The outcomes of college for you are determined by who you are and what you value, the opportunities and environment offered by the institution, and your ability and willingness to engage in the collegiate experience (Astin, 1999).

For some students, the value proposition includes understanding the rigor of the course/class work, the expertise of the faculty in one's major, and the opportunity to engage in undergraduate research. For other students, the value may be centered on the types of jobs students can find post-graduation with a degree from this specific institution. The value proposition may include access to co-curricular involvement in student government, fraternity/sorority life, service and volunteerism, the arts, or study abroad. Graduating early or the ability to take classes online may also be a value proposition. These factors may all be important to you, and you will need to determine if they are available at the institution you choose.

Finally, can you see yourself thriving at the college or university? Not just surviving but actually thriving—learning and growing and developing into a scholar and an adult (Schriener, 2010). You may be the type of student who gets excited by stepping foot on a large university campus in an urban area where there is constant activity. Or you may prefer the more intimate experience of a small college set in a more rural location. Are there courses/classes you want to take, activities and events you want to attend, opportunities for you to engage in new and interesting experiences, services that will meet your needs, and people who will be "good company" (Baxter-Magolda, 2002)? Regardless of your preference, the value proposition is determined by understanding which setting will be best for you and allow you to succeed.

3.2: Determining the Hidden Costs: What You Might Forget!

Whether you went to a public or private high school, you probably didn't think about the costs associated with your education. As you move into adulthood and begin your life as a college student, you will be surprised to learn of all the "hidden" costs that may be yours to manage. No matter which college or university you attend, you will have to think about out-of-pocket expenses. These expenses range from gas for your car, to your favorite name-brand coffee, to late-night take-out, to a cell phone plan, to club dues, clothing, supplies … you get the picture! In Your Turn 3.1, take some time to determine some of your personal out-of-pocket expenses. You can even figure out the weekly cost associated with these expenses and multiply by 30 (the typical number of weeks in a traditional academic year).

YOUR TURN 3.1

Out-of-Pocket Expenses: The Hidden Costs!

Directions: Your financial aid award will assist you in paying for your tuition, fees, room, and meal plan. Whether you reside on campus or commute, you will need to think about additional out-of-pocket expenses that you will incur each year. Some of these expenses depend on your lifestyle and choices while others are just basic items or activities that most college students need to be academically successful. If you check yes to the following questions, you can begin to determine and plan for these costs.

1. Will you be living on campus and bringing a car to campus?

    ___Yes ___No

    •   Check the campus website to determine the cost for registering a vehicle on campus. At some schools it might be free; at others it could be several hundred dollars each semester.

    •   Determine the cost to park on campus. Depending on the campus and the parking locations the fee can vary from no cost to several hundred dollars each semester.

2. Are you commuting to campus?   ___Yes ___No

    •   In addition to parking permits and parking lot or garage fees (see above #1), you will need to calculate the cost of gas to get to and from campus for classes and other activities.

    •   If you are traveling on a toll road or highway, you will also need to determine your daily toll cost.

    •   Car maintenance, over four years, will also be an expense. Oil changes, new tires, and maintenance of your vehicle will need to be considered as you understand how much it will cost you to travel to campus.

3. Do you like to eat out often?   ___Yes ___No

    •   You may have a campus meal plan but if you like to eat out or enjoy a latte you will have additional expenses. Many colleges and universities are situated in cities and towns that cater to the tastes of college students. You will find great dine-in restaurants, take-out restaurants, and restaurants that deliver food right to your door. These expenses can add up quickly. So if you know that you will want to sample the local cuisine, be prepared and plan for these costs.

4. Do you like to look and, more importantly, smell good?

    ___Yes ___No

    • Every student needs personal hygiene items like soap, shampoo, and toothpaste. In addition, you will need to do your laundry which will require laundry detergent and money for the use of the washer and dryer. Some colleges and universities provide free laundry machines, but you will still need detergent. These expenses depend on the brands and products you use every day to stay looking and smelling great!

5. Are you attending a college or university far from your family home?

    ___Yes ___No

    • If you have selected a college or university that requires you to travel home by train, bus, or airplane for holiday or semester breaks, this will be an expense.

6. Do you want to join a sorority or fraternity?   ___Yes ___No

    • Many colleges and universities offer these opportunities. Greek letter organizations charge membership dues each year. You will need to plan for this expense for as long as you are affiliated with the organization.

7. Are you interested in a club sport that the college or university offers?   ___Yes ___No

    • Unlike NCAA athletics, club sports are often funded by the students on the team. Check with the club sport advisor to understand the associated costs.

8. Are you a member of a gym?   ___Yes ___No

    • If you are paying for a local gym, you may want to consider downgrading your membership or ending your contract. Most colleges and universities offer fitness facilities. The cost is in your student fees. If you want to keep your local gym membership, you will need to factor in this expense.

9. Do you pay for your cell phone?   ___Yes ___No

- Check your plan for student discounts. This is a necessary expense that you will need to plan for each month. And you may want to plan for increased data usage as you rely on your phone in different ways in college.

As discussed in the previous section, it is also important to remember that if you take out loans (either private or through Federal Direct loans) you will have to pay them back eventually. Debt repayment can start while you are enrolled in college and most often six months post-graduation. Right now, graduation seems as if it is years and years away, but it will arrive more quickly than you can imagine. You want to make sure that you and your family understand the approximate monthly cost of repayment of all your loans!

3.3: What If I Can't Afford What I Really, Really Want?

After a lot of time reflecting on all the financial information you have and the value proposition, you may still want what you believe you cannot afford. Many students do not always have the luxury of attending their first-choice school. It can be very disappointing. But before you lose hope and must recreate your dream, you can try to appeal your financial aid award.

VOICES FROM CAMPUS 3.2

Marisa

I got into the right school for me. After looking at all my options, I decided a small school was better for me and how I learn. The problem was the school did not offer me enough financial aid. My grandmother recently moved in with my family and between me going to college and my parents caring for her, the expenses are just too much. I know caring for my grandma is important and I felt selfish, but I really wanted to go to this college.

I heard that most financial aid offices are not helpful. A lot of people who graduated last year from my high school talked negatively about their experiences with financial aid. When my mom told me she was going to write a letter asking for more funds, I really thought it was a waste of time. I was surprised when someone from the college called her back. Once they heard my grandma had moved in, they were able to give me some more funds. I'm not sure who was more relieved me, my parents, or my grandma. I'm really glad we asked for a little more help. Now I can go to college and know my family will be okay.

Many times, there are extenuating family circumstances that might necessitate a second review of your financial aid package. You can appeal your financial aid award at each college to which you have been accepted. Financial aid offices read many appeals each year and can determine if the circumstances warrant additional funding for you.

3.4: Steps to Writing a Financial Aid Appeal Letter

Step 1: Address your letter to the specific financial aid administrator that reviews appeals. This information may be listed on the website or may be obtained by calling the financial aid office. Financial aid professionals view themselves as administrators and counselors who provide assistance to families in making their educational and financial decisions. Please allow time for them to review and process the appeal!

Step 2: The tone of your letter should be respectful and appreciative of any funds already offered to you. Remember, the financial aid office is trying to balance the needs of all families, not just yours.

Step 3: Provide any documents demonstrating that your income has been reduced or changed since filing your FAFSA. Talk with the financial aid office to understand if there is specific information that must be completed with the appeal. Information that can be included:

- Loss of a job by a parent or guardian
- Reduction in salary or hours worked by parent or guardian
- Additional dependents living in the house (aging parent or family member not previously listed on your FAFSA)
- Additional income based on a one-time bonus or commission that is not annually given as compensation to parent or guardian
- Funds that are held in trust and cannot be used for educational expenses
- Debt burden due to large medical expenses or losses such as damage to home due to natural disaster (fire, flood, etc.)
- A dependent or family member enrolling in higher education not previously listed on your FAFSA
- Salary based on commission that was higher for the previous year vs. the current year
- Death or divorce of parent or guardian
- One-time cash settlement or inheritance that increased income

Step 4: If you do not have extenuating circumstances, base the appeal on your desire to attend the college or university. You are not and should not bargain with the financial aid administrator. Rather, let them understand your desire to attend their particular school. Sometimes, if the person knows you are willing to get a job on campus and make payments or take out additional loans, they can work with you and your family.

Step 5: If granted any additional funds, follow up with a thank-you card or email. Keep in mind, these same financial aid administrators are there to assist you until graduate.

3.5: Making the Commitment: A BIG Decision!

Once you have worked through your decision-making process, it is time to commit to the college or university that has met your education and financial needs and desires. It is a BIG DEAL and an important decision. You will be required to demonstrate your commitment by submitting an enrollment deposit. This deposit secures your place in the incoming class. It may be a hundred dollars or several hundred dollars. You typically have until May 1 to submit your deposit to guarantee your spot. However, the date by which you submit your deposit could impact housing choices, selection of an orientation date, course/class selection, and other opportunities on campus. You should pay the deposit as soon as you are sure of your decision. Generally, this fee becomes a credit on your first semester bill.

Some colleges and universities require a separate housing deposit. This deposit secures your room on campus. Like the enrollment deposit, it should be submitted as soon as you are sure of your decision, particularly if you have selected a school that has more students who want to live on campus than it has available space. Again, similar to the enrollment deposit, the housing deposit may be credited on your first bill or serve as a security deposit until you leave the residence hall.

There is often an orientation fee that pays for a summer orientation at some point before the start of the semester. These programs will help you make the beginning transitions from high school student to college student. The programs are often mandatory. During orientation, you will most likely plan your course/class schedule, meet faculty in your major department, learn about programs and services offered at the college or university, and meet your new classmates. And so it begins ... your life as a college student!

VOICES FROM CAMPUS 3.3

Xander

I am close to making my decision. I have narrowed it down to two colleges. They both offered me a scholarship but one is a few thousand dollars more than the other. My parents want me to go to the least expensive college. The problem is, I think the one that is a little more expensive has a stronger program in what I want to pursue as a major. They also have a great internship program that may set me up for a future job. It is tough to decide but I need to make my decision soon!

3.6: The Take Away

- A complete picture of the expenses associated with college attendance. While you might be overwhelmed by tuition, room, and board it is important to understand the total cost of attendance so you and your family can financially prepare for the next four years.

- The value proposition for each institution is determined by you—your dreams, your goals, your preferences. You must spend time reflecting on these aspects of the different colleges and universities so you can make an informed, thoughtful choice.

- There are ways to seek out additional resources before abandoning your dream school. Be assertive and ask for help!

Worksheet 3.1: Weighing the Costs

Directions:

In the first column, list the colleges and universities where you have been admitted. Your top-choice school should be listed first and others should follow by preference. In the next column, assign each school a value proposition score ranging from 5 (high value) to 1 (low value). In the third column, list the scholarship or grant funds offered by the college or university. In the fourth column, list the student loan funds included in your financial aid award.

Now compare your rankings with the scholarships and grants offered. Does this change how you feel about your ranking and the value proposition? Does a student or parent loan change your thinking about the school?

Remember scholarships and grants do not have to be repaid. Student loans often need to be repaid six months after you graduate. Repayment of parent loans often begins as soon as you enroll at the college or university.

Use this worksheet to begin the conversation with your parents or guardian regarding the factors in making the right educational and financial decision for you and your family.

College/University Rank	Value Proposition Score (5–1)	Scholarship/Grant Funds	Student Loans
1.			
2.			
3.			
4.			
5.			
6.			
7.			
8.			
9.			
10.			

UNIT II:
THE BUSINESS
OF COLLEGE

THE BASICS

Welcome to college! Congratulations on your great accomplishments. You made it! You are ready to begin this exciting experience. You know you have a terrific opportunity to learn and grow, meet new people, think about new ideas, and be challenged to see life from new perspectives.

It was a complicated journey to figure out the financing for your first year but you and your family did it. You paid your bill and even figured out how to arrive with some spending money in your checking account. You may have been awarded a work-study position or found a part-time, on-campus job so you will have funds coming in on a regular basis.

But the conversation about finances is clearly not over. In this chapter, we will help you understand what types of expenses you can predict and how to create a plan for meeting these expenses. We will also provide you with additional information on obtaining new and different scholarships. When you have financial aid, you also must pay attention to something called Satisfactory Academic Progress, which is explained later in this chapter. Finally, we will introduce you to the many offices on campus which can help you with your financial questions and concerns.

Blake

I was excited to finally figure out how to pay my bill and enroll in college. I met a ton of great people at orientation and classes are going pretty well. I thought I had everything I needed for college but I really didn't think about little stuff. I mean at home when I get in the shower the shampoo and soap are in there! Here I have to buy all that stuff and some things are expensive.

I'm trying really hard to budget my money and I got an on-campus job, but I know I have to be careful about spending. I am learning to think about the difference between what I need and what I want.

4.1: Thinking About Money for College, Again!

Just when you thought you were done thinking about money, you are going to realize that you are not nor can you ever be, during your college experience. Below is a look back at the various expenses you will have during college and how those expenses might change as you pursue your undergraduate degree.

Tuition, Room, Board, and Fees

The cost for tuition, room, board (meals), and fees is evaluated by the college or university on an annual basis. You can expect that as the general cost of living increases for the American public, so will the cost of the expenses for college. Now that you have more knowledge about these expenses, you may be able to make some choices that can reduce the costs. For example, your institution may have a variety of living options and meal plans.

After your first year in college, you may have a better idea of how many meals you actually will eat in the campus dining facilities. Are you not utilizing your meal plan to its fullest? Are you using your flexible dollars on campus or eating off campus for many of your meals? Are you not eating breakfast or skipping a meal due to class schedules or activities? Reducing your meal plan costs reduces your overall college costs. You may also want to reevaluate your living situation. There may be less expensive options on campus!

Textbooks

After your first trip to the campus bookstore, you now understand the real cost of academic textbooks. It is essential to have the assigned textbook for the class so you can keep up with the reading and assignments. Many times, the professor will not "teach from the book" and expects that you come prepared having read the assigned chapters.

There are many ways to gain access to your textbooks. You can purchase both new and used textbooks from your campus bookstore. New books will be the most expensive and used copies will be less. Often the used copies have been highlighted or marked up. If you do not find these markings distracting, you can save some money on your books!

You can also find an online seller and purchase both new and used versions. Often, students in previous classes look to sell their textbooks and advertise on bulletin boards or online platforms. A new way to gain access to textbooks at a lower cost is to rent them from your campus bookstore or online seller. Another option is to ask your instructor if they have put a copy of the textbook on reserve at the library. If the book is on reserve, you most likely have to read it in the library as opposed to taking it with you. This reserve system has dual benefits to you—you can save your money and structure your time to get your reading done without distraction!

Technology

You most likely arrived with your own cell phone. Some students do not realize they may use their data differently on campus than they did in high school. To ensure that you have enough data and are not subject to overage charges, you may want to adjust your data plan. Contact your wireless phone provider to understand how you can reduce your bill and get the best coverage necessary for your new lifestyle.

You may have come to campus with your own computer and printer. Your fees most likely include computer and printing services. Typically, students are allotted a certain page amount of printing per week. One small way to save money is to use that allocation for which you have already paid before using your own paper and ink. Your institution may also have available the latest software for you to download to your personal computer for free or at a reduced cost. Check with your office of information services to understand what products they may offer to you.

Transportation and Parking

If you brought a car to campus or if you are commuting to campus, you already know that you have expenses related to parking, driving, and maintaining your automobile. Campus enforcement of parking is a given at most institutions, and illegally parked cars are ticketed and towed. To not incur these expenses, make sure you are following all the instructions and signage about parking.

If you do not have access to a car, you are relying on other types of transportation. If you are commuting, you may want to see if there is a carpool program at your institution. If you are living on campus, you can certainly make use of ride sharing, public transportation, taxi services, and the kindness of friends with cars. Many institutions have car sharing programs and some have free bike share programs. Make sure to check out your college or university website to explore these options.

Living Expenses

It is expensive to be a college student, especially from the perspective of the college student. If you are living at home, you may be fortunate enough to not have to pay for your living expenses—but it is always nice to offer! If you are living on campus, you may have to pay for everything on your own. You are realizing that it costs a lot of money to do your laundry!

We often underestimate our living expenses and we often do not plan for unexpected expenses. You can create a small savings account to have access to funds when needed. You may want to purchase a sweatshirt at the bookstore, a gift for a friend, celebrate your accomplishments, go to the movies, or participate in an activity. Having some funds in reserve allows you to be able to say YES!

Living off Campus

Many colleges and universities require first-year, first-time students to either live on campus or commute from home. But if you have an opportunity to live off campus in an apartment or house, either in your first year or subsequent years, you will need to be mindful of the many expenses that come with your choice. You will need to pay rent. Utilities (gas, electric, water, trash removal) may or may not be included. You will need to pay for cable and/or Internet access. You will need to provide all that you need to live comfortably—food, cooking utensils, furniture, toilet paper, etc.

For a more detailed discussion about the expenses of living on your own in an off-campus location, please refer to Chapter 7.

4.2: Financial Aid: Not Just One and Done!

The good news is you have figured out paying for your first year of college. The reality is you will need to figure it out for the next three years or until your graduation. The FAFSA must be filed annually and your financial aid award will change as your family and circumstances change. A sibling or parent/ guardian enrolling in college or university may actually increase your award. A sibling or parent/guardian graduating from college may decrease your award. Your award will also change as your family's income changes. The most important thing to remember is to file the FAFSA each year as early as you can since some states have due dates for funding.

Below are some other points to keep in mind as you advance in your first year as an undergraduate:

4.3: Scholarships: A Second Look

Many colleges and universities receive gifts from alumni donors to support students. These are often in the form of scholarships. Some colleges and universities generally set up an application process for students to apply for these scholarships. Others may add them to the financial aid award. And others may reach out to individual students with scholarship opportunities that match their specific situations.

Sometimes the alumni donor has restricted the gift to specific majors, interests, financial need, or GPA. Some donors want the funds to go to a student from a specific region of the state or country. Other donors are interested in funding students who exhibit leadership or service work. The bottom line is you should apply for any scholarships funded by your institutional advancement or foundation office when you meet the criteria. You can typically explore these scholarships online. You can search for these offices on your college or university website. Scholarships may be listed on a few departmental Web pages such as alumni affairs and institutional fundraising/development. You can also ask your financial aid office about endowed scholarship opportunities.

4.4: Maintaining Your Awards and Scholarships

In the beginning of this book we talked about merit scholarships. If you receive a scholarship from your college or university, you will need to meet certain academic benchmarks to retain the funds for the following year. It is important to know the cumulative grade point average needed each year to continue to receive this scholarship. If you are unsure, then visit or email the financial aid office and they will be able to let you know the requirements to maintain your award. It is your responsibility to make sure you achieve and maintain the grade point average required. Remember, both semesters will be averaged into the cumulative GPA requirement so both fall and spring semesters count. If you have a multi-year scholarship, your continued cumulative GPA will be an important parameter for keeping the scholarship.

4.5: New Scholarship Opportunities

Now that you are on campus you are going to hear and read about scholarship opportunities all over campus. Within your academic department there may be some funding for students to work on research or travel funding. The campus newspaper may have information regarding scholarship opportunities from a variety of people and organizations. Your college or university may send information out by email when scholarships become available. Read your campus email, read the campus newspaper, and check out departmental bulletin boards frequently for scholarship announcements. Whenever you see an opportunity to apply for funding, take the risk and apply. As we said in the previous chapters, the deadlines matter so plan to submit your materials a week in advance of any posted deadline and submit everything requested including official college or university transcripts. This takes time and willingness to take a risk, but any additional funds will only help you long term. Bonus: Any scholarships you receive should go on your résumé!

4.6: Satisfactory Academic Progress (SAP)

Each college or university is required by the United States Department of Education to monitor all students to ensure they are making satisfactory academic progress or SAP as it is called in most campus financial aid offices. Okay, hold on, here is the technical meaning of SAP:

> SAP means that a student maintains progress to their degree in order to receive financial aid. To measure progress, financial aid offices evaluate a student's academic record at the completion of each semester or each academic year. They review both the quantitative (maximum time frame and completion rate) and the qualitative (cumulative grade point average) as a student pursues their degree. Failure to meet these standards will result in the suspension of financial aid eligibility which may include federal, state, and institutional aid.

Here is what you need to know: SAP means you must take and complete a specific number of credits and receive grades in these courses/classes that keep you on track to graduate. You must maintain a certain GPA and earn a certain amount of credits to be making SAP. Your college or university will have their guidelines listed on the financial aid website.

While on the surface this sounds like no big deal, there are some ways to be at risk of not making SAP that are important to know. Most colleges allow you to drop and add courses/classes at the beginning of each semester during drop/add period. This will not affect SAP if you do it during this time frame. Colleges and universities also allow students to withdraw from courses/classes during the semester, in some cases many weeks into the semester. This is where an SAP issue can occur.

Students who repeatedly withdraw from courses/classes can have a progression issue or a completion rate issue. Additionally, withdrawal from classes for an entire semester will impact your SAP. Finally, if you fail a course/class, you don't get any credit for that course/class as an "F" grade equals zero credits earned—another progression issue.

Satisfactory Academic Progress also considers your grade point average. Your college or university will have grade point average requirements to continue enrollment. To be safe, you want to keep your GPA above a 2.0 each semester. What should you do?

✔ Be thoughtful when you and your academic advisor plan your schedule. If you know you cannot manage two courses/classes that are challenging for you, such as calculus and physics, in one semester be up-front about what you can manage.

✔ If you must take a couple of challenging courses/classes together, get help from a tutor early in the semester so you get the best grade possible and remain in the course/class.

✔ Consider taking those difficult courses/classes during the summer to lighten your course/class load and during a time when you can focus on one or two courses/classes rather than five or six.

✔ Only withdraw from any course/class if you absolutely must. Limit course/class withdrawals over your four years as an undergraduate. Doing so will help you stay in compliance with SAP.

✔ If you have to withdraw from a course/class or from the semester, check with your financial aid office to understand how withdrawal will affect your financial aid for the semester and moving forward.

Sandra

Everyone told me college was harder than high school, but I figured I got good grades in high school without doing much homework or even reading the books. I mean I had above a 3.2 my senior year and studied about two hours a week. I just paid attention in class and got my grades. I thought just going to class in college would be enough. Boy, was I wrong!

For my first exam I had not done all the reading because I thought my class notes would be what we were tested on. Big mistake! About half of the test must have been from the reading because I did not know the answers to those questions. When I got my exam back and saw that big "F" at the top of it I felt like a total failure. It made going to the class really hard, because I felt embarrassed. I started making up excuses not to go, which left me falling further and further behind. Before I knew it, finals were just around the corner.

I went to get a tutor and thought I could do really well on the final and at least get a "C." The tutor helped me, but we both knew I needed tutoring all semester. I'm so sorry I didn't listen to everyone, including my parents who told me I needed to study every day in college. I know my grades are going to be horrible and my parents are going to be upset.

My academic advisor told me I may have not made Satisfactory Academic Progress which means my financial aid might be taken away from me. She said I would get a letter from financial aid about my failure to maintain SAP. I'm scared about getting the letter. I don't know what to do. I just know I learned a lot from failing this class and I want a second chance to do better. I hope there is a way.

4.7: No Satisfactory Academic Progress: Now What?

If you receive notification from the financial aid office that you have not met their SAP requirements, you can appeal the decision in writing and sometimes in person. You should be candid and honest about what negatively impacted your semester or year. If something traumatic has happened in your family, you need to let the financial aid staff know what occurred.

Maybe you had an ongoing or long-term health issue that prevented you from getting to class. In either of these cases you should provide documentation of a family or personal medical issue. If you simply were not prepared for the rigors of college work, you should let them know what you are prepared to do to get on track. Ways you can work at making SAP could include meeting with a tutor on a regular basis, visiting the writing center, retaking courses/classes to improve your grade point average, and taking summer classes to add to your credits. Your plan should be detailed and specific. Remember SAP is a federal or state requirement. If you are offered a second chance to keep your financial aid, you need to demonstrate that you are willing to work hard with a realistic plan to do so.

4.8: Help on Campus

One of the more frequent comments heard on a college campus is, "I wish I knew that [particular service] existed." There are so many offices and faculty/staff who are available to help students navigate the complexities of college. Each college or university has services to meet the needs of their specific student population. Below is an overview of some offices and their functions that are common on most campuses. The staff in these offices can help you think through issues related to finances. You can visit your campus website to learn more about services available to students.

YOUR TURN 4.1

Your Guide to YOUR Campus Resources

Directions: The staff on your campus want to help you navigate your finances and answer questions for you throughout your college career. The worksheet below is designed for you to fill in important contact information for key offices and people on your campus who might have connection with issues that arise around finances and funding your college experience. This worksheet can serve as a reference for you so you know who to contact with questions and concerns. You should update it each fall when you return to campus.

Office	Phone and Website	Staff Person/Email	Office Location
Financial Aid Office			
Bursar/Cashier Office			
Bookstore			
Student Employment or Human Resources			
The Career Development Center			
Academic Advising/ Student Success Center/ Academic Advisor			
The Registrar's Office			
Institutional Advancement/ Foundation			
Student Affairs			

Financial Aid

Throughout this book, the financial aid office is mentioned as the "go to" service on campus. It is the office where you can find answers to your questions about financial aid, work-study, FAFSA completion, and anything else related to financing your college career. It should be the first office you visit with your questions. They will have the most knowledge to direct you to the resources you need.

Bursar

The Bursar's office is the office on campus that issues your semester bill. They also collect funds for many other types of bills and debts such as judicial fines, parking fines, etc. The Bursar's office can help you understand your bill. They can also direct you to resources on campus if there are concerns about meeting the obligations of your bill.

Bookstore

As discussed earlier, the campus bookstore may have many options available to gain access to textbooks. At the end of the semester, campus bookstores often have a service to buy back your textbooks. You will not get what you paid for them but you will most likely get something!

Academic Advising, Student Success Center, or Your Academic Advisor

No, the academic advising center will not be able to give you any money. Nor will your academic advisor! But what they can do is to help you plan your courses/classes and schedule in the best way for you to maintain Satisfactory Academic Progress. You should contact your advisor when you believe you need or want to withdraw from a class. They will be able to help you weigh the benefits and liabilities of doing so at that particular time. They can also direct you to tutoring and student support resources.

Career Development Center

Most colleges and universities have a career development center. At larger institutions, the career development center may be located in your college where your major is housed. The career development center offers a myriad of services and resources for job searching and interviewing, but they also may offer access to off-campus, part-time job opportunities. Find the career development center on your college or university website and see what services they offer!

Student Employment Center or Human Resources

Depending on your campus, a student employment center or human resources office will have access to on-campus job opportunities. You will also turn in documents (W-2, I-9) and forms so that you can be paid for your on-campus employment. Staff in this office may be able to offer you suggestions about the various types of on-campus employment.

Registrar's Office

The Registrar's office is the office that houses student records. The staff in this office can help you obtain your official and unofficial transcript, help you understand Satisfactory Academic Progress, process any transfer credits, and answer questions about scheduling.

Institutional Advancement/Foundation/Alumni Affairs

Where scholarships are housed depends on the individual campus but most often one of these offices can at least direct you to scholarship information. This office might also know about very particular scholarship opportunities that might match your individual and unique qualifications and circumstances.

Student Affairs

The office of student affairs is designed to help students in all areas of the college experience, especially in those areas outside of the classroom. The staff in student affairs understand the developmental needs of students. They know how to help you figure out how to navigate your individual campus community and where to go on campus for additional help.

VOICES FROM CAMPUS 4.3

Xander

I cannot believe I am in college. It is great and I am learning a lot about myself and how to navigate my classes, studying, living with a roommate, my work-study job on campus, and taking care of myself. I feel like I have enough money saved to get through the semester but I am unsure about the spring semester.

At orientation, the staff talked about our financial aid awards but honestly it was information overload those few days. The presentation was kind of lost on me. I am pretty sure I will be okay in terms of money. At least I hope so!

4.9: The Take Away

- Most students are never done figuring out the financing for their college education. Remember, you need to complete the FAFSA and any additional documentation every academic year and as early in the academic year as possible.
- There are ways to find additional savings and financing as you progress through your undergraduate career. Take advantage of all opportunities!
- Maintain Satisfactory Academic Progress. If you are not able to do so, ask for help!
- Ask for help—we can't emphasize this enough. There are people and resources available to help you be successful!

BEYOND THE BASICS: THE HIDDEN COSTS

" **I** learned so much about myself outside of the classroom" is a very common refrain from college students who make a commitment to engage in co-curricular and extracurricular activities. And this is very true. In fact, there is strong relationship between involvement and success (Astin, 1999; Gallup-Purdue, 2014). Engagement in experiences outside of the classroom takes time and often there are associated expenses. The value of engagement is clear, but you will want to understand the hidden costs and then make a clear decision.

YOUR TURN 5.1

168 Hours

Twenty-four hours in a day and seven days in a week equals 168 hours in a week. How will you spend your time? Time management is often a challenge for college students, especially first-year students. In high school, your time was very scheduled but in college you often have a lot of unplanned and unscheduled time. One reason students give for not engaging in opportunities is that they do not have time. As you choose your co-curricular activities you want to weigh the value of the opportunity against the associated costs and time. This exercise will help you understand how much time you do have throughout the week.

Step 1: Fill in the calendar with your existing time commitments. Make sure to consider the following activities:

- ✔ Classes
- ✔ Sleep (6–7 hours per night)
- ✔ Eating (at least 1 hour per day)
- ✔ Studying (at least 5 hours per course/class)

Step 2: Now consider and add other activities such as:

- ✔ Exercise
- ✔ Employment
- ✔ Travel time (if you are off campus or a commuter)

Step 3: Are you surprised by the time that is left on the schedule? Consider filling some of your time with co-curricular involvement. Just make sure to consider the actual costs and the opportunity costs along the way!

Time of Day	Monday	Tuesday	Wednesday	Thursday	Friday	Saturday	Sunday
7 am–8 am							
8 am–9 am							
9 am–10 am							
10 am–11 am							
11 am–12 pm							
12 pm–1 pm							
1 pm–2 pm							
2 pm–3 pm							
3 pm–4 pm							
4 pm–5 pm							
5 pm–6 pm							
6 pm–7 pm							
7 pm–8 pm							
8 pm–9 pm							
9 pm–10 pm							
10 pm–11 pm							
11 pm–12am							
12 am–6 am							

There are many free and low-cost opportunities for involvement on campus. It is important to take advantage of these options throughout your college experience. You will learn new information, meet new people, have fun, and feel connected to your institution. Not every experience on campus is easily affordable or free. This chapter will introduce you to the more popular co-curricular and extracurricular opportunities that add value to your education but come at a financial cost. It is important to understand the expenses that are associated with these experiences and then weigh the value proposition.

5.1: Bon Voyage: Study Abroad and Travel Programs

Traveling to another country can be life-changing! Most colleges offer opportunities to study and learn in a country outside of the United States. These opportunities can be short-term trips for a week to 10 days or longer term for a summer or even a full semester. Learning about and living in another country, even for a week, can provide you with a deeper appreciation for a new culture and will be attractive to many employers after you graduate. Understanding how to navigate life in a different country, including communicating in a new language and learning about the history and culture of the country, will enhance your appreciation of the global community.

Travel programs come at a cost. These are probably costs that you did not plan for when thinking about your finances for college. Additional expenses include the cost of a passport, plane ticket, housing, meals, insurance (travel or health), transportation in the country, and other excursions. If your college offers the experience for credit, you will also need to pay for the credits or tuition. Depending on where you go and the length of the trip these costs can vary. A week-long trip to Mexico might be several thousand dollars while a semester in England might be significantly more.

To determine which experiences might fit into your budget, start by visiting the global studies or study abroad office on your campus. The staff in these offices can help you explore the different types of travel programs offered by and through your college. They may even suggest alternative programs offered at other colleges and universities. The staff often have information about how you can obtain funds to offset the cost of your travel through the college, outside scholarships, and other funding sources. If you are traveling for credit, your financial aid may help cover some of the cost of your trip.

After all your investigation, if you decide you can afford to have a travel experience as part of your undergraduate experience, establish a realistic budget for all your personal and travel expenses. Keep in mind the country to which you are traveling may have a different currency. Do not forget to convert U.S. dollars into that currency to be sure you are budgeting (and spending) appropriately!

Travel opportunities are unique experiences in higher education. If you are fortunate enough to be able to afford this kind of experience, make sure you are doing everything you can to immerse yourself in the culture. Try new foods, explore museums, attend cultural events, and meet the local people. Travel experiences in college often lead students to a lifetime of travel and an appreciation of being a global citizen.

VOICES FROM CAMPUS 5.1

Katie

I was excited to learn I could spend a semester in London studying economics. My long-term goal is to work in a global business that allows me to travel for my job, so this opportunity was perfect for me! I set up a meeting with the office of global studies to figure out how to apply for the program and learn about the expenses associated with going to London. I had not really considered all the costs.

I've traveled before but only with my family ... I guess I did not know how expensive a plane ticket and living expenses could be in a major city. My financial aid will cover the credits I will earn for the semester so that part is done. I am glad I met with the global studies staff person a year in advance. It will take me that long to save for the trip.

I've taken an extra job this summer too. I don't have a lot of time to hang out with friends this summer but this is a once-in-a-lifetime experience and I am willing to make some sacrifices. Once I get to London, my goal is to see and do as much as I can for the entire semester. I can't wait to eat fish and chips, ride a double-decker bus, and explore the city!

5.2: It Is All Greek to Me: Fraternity/Sorority Life

You may have heard about fraternities and sororities and are thinking about joining one. Greek life experiences are available on many, but not all, college campuses across the country. Fraternities and sororities often are connected to a national office that oversees the individual campus chapter. Greek life provides many wonderful experiences in leadership, service, philanthropy, and networking. When you join a fraternity or sorority, you will meet other students and share the values of the organization with which you affiliate. You will also have the opportunity, if the organization is a national Greek letter organization, to attend conferences and meet other members from across the country. Once you graduate, this network may help you find a job. If you move to a new city you can often connect with alumni of your organization and meet other members in the region.

Joining a fraternity or sorority comes at a financial cost. You will need to carefully consider these expenses as you think about membership in Greek life. The costs start immediately and continue throughout your involvement. Once you are invited to join and complete a period of new member educa-tion, you will be expected to pay membership expenses. The membership expenses will continue each year you are enrolled in college. If you choose to stay involved as an alumni member, there are membership dues that are collected annually by the chapter.

The process of becoming a member of a fraternity or sorority varies from campus to campus. Generally, there is a new membership recruitment period in the fall or spring semester. This recruitment period will allow you to visit with current fraternity and sorority members to understand more about the specific organization, their activities, and their values. Some chapters are very focused on community service, others are focused on academic achievement, while still others are focused on the social life of their members.

You will want to find out if the current members' values align with yours and if you have the grade point average, extracurricular experiences, and other attributes the fraternity or sorority is seeking.

As a new member, you will need to dedicate both time and money. You will learn about the time commitment and new member fees as well as ongoing annual membership dues during the recruitment period. You also will want to inquire about other expenses such as clothing, pins, travel, and additional dues. These costs can vary from a few hundred dollars to several thousand dollars depending on which organization you join.

The office of student leadership or Greek life office can help you understand which chapters exist on your campus. The staff will guide students through the recruitment process and inform them of the policies associated with fraternity and sorority life on campus. There are GPA requirements to maintain your membership. There are policies about new member education, social activities, and the amount of community service each chapter is required to do each semester.

5.3: Let's Play Ball: Club and Intramural Sports

Intercollegiate athletics are offered at many campuses across the country. Separate from intercollegiate athletics, club sports allow students the opportunity to participate in a sport that may not be offered through intercollegiate athletics. Club sports also give students an opportunity to compete and play for fun and exercise. Club sport involvement can help you meet other students who share your passion for your sport.

Club sports are typically student organizations recognized by the college or university. They often receive funding to offset travel, equipment, or field time. At some institutions, students pay for the expenses associated with playing on a club sport team each semester they participate. The team will engage in fundraising efforts to offset expenses. Depending on which sport you play the associated costs could be modest or require a more significant financial commitment. You will want to determine the cost to play and to travel. You will also need to consider the expense of your equipment.

Once you know this information you can decide if playing a club sport is right for you. The campus recreation office can help you understand what club sports are offered or how to start a new club sport organization on your campus.

5.4: Taking It to the Streets: Alternative Spring Break and Service Trips

"Spring Break" is an age-old tradition for college students. Typically, the break occurs in mid-March and many "Spring-Breakers" head to popular vacation spots for a week of socializing with other college students. It goes without saying that there are many costs associated with this vacation plan. Some students head home or, if allowed, stay on campus—a much more affordable option.

Alternative Spring Break trips have become quite popular with college students. Instead of heading to a vacation spot or just catching up on sleep, students embark on college-sponsored volunteer service trips for the week. Typically, students begin their experience with leadership training on campus prior to the trip. Students will travel to an area, either in or out of the country, to volunteer in home rehabilitation, community clean-up efforts, assistance to residents in the community, etc. These trips are wonderful, enriching opportunities for students and allow for bonding with others.

There are costs associated with service trips. Most organizations will engage in fundraising throughout the year so that some expenses are covered. You should be prepared to pay for your own food, clothing, personal items, and entertainment. The college or university will most likely provide transportation. Most significantly, you should take into account the opportunity cost. Can you afford to sacrifice a week of wages?

Demonstrating your commitment to community service can be a great addition to your résumé and your undergraduate experience. You will learn about yourself and about others in your community. You will certainly develop an understanding of the importance of giving back to the community and helping others. Employers often seek out employees who are going to enhance the workplace and the community in which they live. If you are thinking about engaging in service, an alternative Spring Break trip is a good place to start. Who knows? You may return from your break with a lifelong commitment to helping others!

5.5: Internships and Clinical Experiences

Many undergraduate majors require internships or clinical experiences as part of the curriculum/course of study. These off-campus opportunities allow you to take what you learn in the classroom and apply it in your field. You are probably not surprised to learn that students preparing to be teachers or social workers will be required to complete a year of student teaching or practical experience in a clinical setting. Many other majors will require these types of practical and applied experiences. Other majors will suggest that you complete an internship, even if it is not for credit. This real-world work experience will help you learn the skills of your intended profession. Internships will enhance your résumé and may assist you in your job search post-graduation.

Internships and clinical experiences come with costs beyond the cost of tuition. Below is a list of expenses to consider as you plan for a credit or non-credit internship.

Transportation

Typically, your college or university will NOT provide transportation to the internship site. You will need to consider the expense of getting yourself back and forth to the site. You may need to buy or borrow a car. You can consider public transportation if available. Some academic departments may help students form car pools so students can share the transportation expenses of gas and possible tolls.

Food

If you are spending the entire day at an internship site, you are going to be hungry! If you purchased a meal plan at school, you may not have thought about the cost of food throughout the day. It is easy to spend a lot of money on breakfast, coffee, lunch, and snacks in just one day! You want to think through these expenses. If you did purchase a meal plan, you can inquire about obtaining a bag lunch to pick up in the morning before you leave campus. Many food service providers offer bag lunches or dinners for students who cannot utilize their meal plans during the day.

Clothing

The clothes you throw on to go to class may not be the clothes you can wear at your internship site. You may need to invest in more professional clothing. You may be required to wear a uniform if you are in a clinical setting such as a hospital. It is important to ask your internship supervisor about the dress code before you begin your internship experience.

Liability Insurance

Some internship sites might require you to purchase liability insurance. If the internship is part of your course/class requirements, the faculty will let you know if you need to purchase any insurance. If you are doing a non-credit internship, you may want to ask if you need to purchase your own insurance. Many internships will not require it but it will be important to you to know if you need to account for this expense.

Opportunity Cost

Internships and clinical experiences, especially if they are part of your curriculum, are often unpaid. This means that the hours you are at your internship you are not able to be at a work-study job or other type of employment. You will want to consider the opportunity cost of engaging in an internship. Working in the summer and over breaks is one way to make up for lost work hours. Budgeting your student loan dollars is another way to make up for the money you would earn at a part-time job.

Maria

My professor told me about an internship opportunity at a business in my hometown for the summer. I'm interested in interior design so the experience would really add to what I have learned in my course/class work. The owner has done work in both home and business settings so I will learn which kind of design work is right for me when I graduate. Sounds great, right? It is, and I am super excited but the downside is I will not be paid. I talked it through with my mom and dad this spring because it means I will have to find a summer job at night. I cannot afford to not work, and the internship offers me real-life experience. So during my summer "vacation" I will be working 8:30 a.m.–4:30 p.m. as an intern and then waitressing nights and weekends. It's going to be tough, but I think it will pay off when I start a job search after graduation!

5.6: Conferences and Educational Off-Campus Experiences

As you progress through your college experience, you may be asked to attend a professional conference in your major or a leadership experience through your co-curricular involvement. Often the college or university will assist you in paying for the experience and may even help with transportation—but not always! You will want to consider all the costs before agreeing to participate. There are predictable costs such as registration fees and travel/lodging expenses. You will want to know if meals and entertainment are included. You may need to wear professional clothing. Ask about the dress code! And, once again, you should think about missed wages from your employment.

Xander

I visited the career center on campus because graduation is getting closer. I heard that the staff in the center can be very helpful. In order to make my résumé stand out I need to think about doing something distinctive such as study abroad or an internship. I've had campus jobs and summer jobs, but the career center staff told me I need experience directly related to my major. It makes sense to me. So I am going to start applying for study abroad programs and internships to see what is out there that makes sense. I know it will be another expense, but I've got to give it a shot!

5.7: The Take Away

- There are many wonderful opportunities in college but often these opportunities come at a cost.
- You may have to limit your experiences based on your personal financial situation.
- Evaluate the costs of these experiences before agreeing to participate.
- Weigh the opportunity cost of participation. There are often long-term benefits associated with participation in these out-of-class experiences.
- If your program of study requires an internship or clinical experience, start planning for the expenses and possible loss of wages now.

6

HELP WANTED: FINDING EMPLOYMENT DURING COLLEGE

Twenty-five percent of college students are working full time while enrolled full time in school, and 40 percent of undergraduates are working at least 30 hours a week (Carnevale, Smith, Melton, & Price, 2015). The economic realities of higher education mean that most students must work while attending college, at least part time. Maybe you had a part-time job while in high school. Great! You understand how to get a job and keep a job. And you enjoyed the "fruits" of your labor—money, experience, skills development, friends, to name a few.

Whether you had a job or not, this chapter will provide you with some general information about how to prepare for a job search, what types of jobs might be available on your campus, and how to find a job off campus if you prefer. You will also learn about what types of jobs to pursue during your winter and summer breaks. Working while in college is possible and in many ways will enhance your college experience. Just like in high school, a job in college will provide you with money, experience, skills, and hopefully new colleagues and friends.

6.1: First Things First: Preparing for Finding a Job

Preparation is key when looking for a job! The job search requires thought and work. The good news is that most colleges and universities have staff to help you with your job search whether it be for a part-time job while in college or for full-time employment post-graduation. First things first. Find the career development center on your campus. The career development center will have many resources, including staff to help you as you prepare to find a job. They can help you craft a résumé and cover letter, talk with you about appropriate interview attire, and help you prepare for the interview. They may also have listings of part-time employment that you can pursue.

You will need a few "tools" to help you in your job search. Below is a discussion of these "tools" for you to explore.

YOUR TURN 6.1

Preparing for the Job Search

To start any job search you will need to be prepared. The following checklist provides information for you to prepare as you begin the job search. Some items you may need to develop and others you may need to locate so you can give a prospective employer everything they need to hire you.

Item	Explanation	Suggestions	Resources
Résumé	One-page résumé of past work experience	Draft a sample and have several people proofread it for errors.	The career development center
List of references	3–5 former teachers or former employers that can speak to your experience	Notify all references in advance for their permission to use them as a reference and for current contact information.	
Email account	Your personal email	Create a new email for your job search. It should be professional and use your name. Example: SarahSmith123@gmail.com.	Gmail, Yahoo mail, etc.

Item	Explanation	Suggestions	Resources
Documents	For a business to cut you a paycheck you will need to complete a tax form called a W-9 form.	Have a state driver's license, social security card, birth certificate, and/or passport with you once you obtain a job. Employers can only use original documents for these requirements and cannot pay you until they receive them.	Your parents or family may have these in a safe place in your home.
An interview outfit	You want attire that is clean, pressed, and professional for interviews.	You do not need a suit in most cases, but you do want to appear professional. Avoid tight or revealing clothing.	Your closet
Class schedule	Employers will want to know when you are available to work.	Make sure you add additional time to get from campus to your job using your car, feet, or public transportation.	
Academic calendar	Employers will want to know when each semester begins and ends.	If you know you will not be able to work during final exams or over breaks, let the employer know.	On the college or university website
Personal appearance	Until you know an employer's policy, it is best to cover tattoos and piercings.	It is okay to ask about a campus or company policy regarding tattoos and body piercings.	May be listed on the college or company website under human resource policies or employee handbook.

Résumé and Cover Letter

Your résumé is a document that lists your experience. Most likely you can keep your résumé to one page. You will want to list important experiences you have had such as employment, volunteer opportunities, any awards or scholarships you received, and any club or student organization involvement. You might also want to list special skills you possess. For example, bilingual proficiency, social media skills, computer skills, etc. Your résumé can also include the names and contact information of references. Your references should include people who know your work and should not be people who are related to you!

You will also want to draft a cover letter. The cover letter introduces you to the potential employer and gives you a chance to explain why you are interested in the position. You can also have a shorter letter that you might use in an email where you would attach your résumé. The staff at the career development center can help you structure and refine both documents.

Proper Attire

Let's face it … at some point in your college career you will have to go on an interview. You will need to present yourself to a potential employer in the best light possible. If you are invited to meet with someone for an interview, you want to make sure that you do not just drop in after your gym workout. Make sure you come dressed in an appropriate manner for that office. You do not have to spend any money to purchase new clothes for this interview. Make sure though that your clothes are neat, clean, and not too revealing. Later in your undergraduate career, as you interview for internships and professional positions, you will want to get advice on professional interviewing attire.

Interviewing Skills

It is important to have some understanding of how to participate in an interview. The interviewer will ask you questions, but you should give more than yes/no answers. A good interviewer will ask you questions that do not require just a yes or no answer, but remember to expand on the answers you give. Also, as important as answering questions, you will also be evaluated on the questions you ask. Come prepared to ask questions about the position. For example, you might ask, "What is something I can learn through my employment here?" or "Why do students like working in this office?"

Another interview tip is to make sure you learn as much as you can about the office before coming to the interview. You can find out a lot of information by accessing the department's website and talking with others on campus.

6.2: Finding a Job on Campus

An on-campus job has many benefits. First, you are on the campus and can often come and go from class, to meals, and to your job with very little effort. Second, your employer understands that you are a college student and might have to adapt your schedule based on exams, projects, etc. Third, you will get to know a lot about how the campus functions and get to know faculty and staff outside of the classroom. Often, students can keep their on-campus job for their entire college career, although many students prefer to vary their employment sites if possible.

There are many different types of on-campus employment to explore. Below are discussion and access information about the various types of on-campus employment.

Federal Work-Study

As discussed in previous chapters, federal work-study is part of your financial aid package. When you receive your financial aid award, you will be notified if you have received work-study. You will be assigned to an office or service and given instructions on how to report for the first day. You will have a supervisor who will help you understand the work of the office and the tasks you will be doing. Most work-study students receive a paycheck. You can choose to use these funds to offset your personal or academic expenses. Most work-study jobs are 10–15 hours per week. As mentioned above, some students have the same work-study position for their entire college experience.

Because work-study is attached to your financial aid, the number of hours you are eligible to work may change each year. If you are not awarded work-study or your eligibility changes, you can contact the office of financial aid and ask them to reconsider your award. At some institutions, you may be limited to the number of jobs you can have on campus. If you have a work-study position, you may not be eligible for additional on-campus employment. Check with the office of financial aid.

Other On-Campus Employment

There are jobs on campus that are not connected to the federal work-study program. Often colleges and universities will list their employment opportunities on an electronic portal through the human resources office, financial aid office, or the career development center. Some employers may use the student newspaper, student emails, or just plain word of mouth! Below are some suggestions for where to pursue on-campus employment.

Dining Services

Okay, we know that most students do not want to work in their school dining hall but there are many benefits. First, the work is steady and you know that you will always get hours. Second, you will see a lot of your friends as they come in to have their meals. Third, some of your meals may be included! Also, dining services is not just covering the dining hall during meals. Students often find employment with the catering department of dining services. There are a lot of benefits to this position too. Yes, you get to eat but you are often in the company of a lot of campus leaders. You may even get to serve a dignitary or VIP who comes to campus for a speaking engagement or event. Many of these events are on the weekends and evenings and may not conflict with your class schedule.

Campus Bookstore

The campus bookstore may or may not have steady employment for students but it is worth finding out. Stop in and ask about possible employment. They may also have "seasonal" work at the busy times before and during the semester. You may even receive a discount from the bookstore to apply to your textbooks or campus swag!

Offices on Campus

Offices on campus may hire students to assist in the delivery of services or with logistical tasks. They may use the campus website to post opportunities or they may advertise through formal or informal networks. Do not hesitate to ask around campus to understand if employment opportunities exist. For example, if you are in the library frequently, ask the person at the desk if they are hiring. The worst thing they can tell you is that they are not, but they may know of other employment on campus!

You can also seek various desk assistant positions. As you travel around campus, look at where there are students staffing offices and information centers. For example, many residence halls have desk staff to answer questions and manage the mailroom, requests for keys, access to computer and game rooms, etc. Student unions often have students staffing their information desks. Computer centers, welcome centers, libraries, etc. may all hire students to assist with staffing.

Faculty Research Assistants

These positions often go to graduate assistants who are pursing advanced degrees. But it does not hurt to ask your professor if they have any openings for a research assistant. If they announce that they are hiring a research assistant, apply! This type of employment will give you excellent experience and a paycheck.

Paraprofessional Positions

Paraprofessional student positions are varied throughout the institutions. These positions may be found in many student service and student affairs departments. They come with a lot of responsibilities to serve other students. Students must apply for these positions and they often undergo a rigorous interview process. Typically, there is a training period that occurs during the summer right before the start of the semester and often throughout the school year. Examples of paraprofessional experiences include resident assistant, orientation leader, tutor, peer educator/mentor, student union assistant, and university ambassador (tour guide). The compensation varies depending on the position. Resident assistant positions often come with a free room and a stipend.

These positions are highly sought after by students. They are often filled by upperclassmen who have had some experience at the institution. These positions are difficult to obtain for first-semester, first-year students. But if you are interested in a paraprofessional position, you can begin to explore in your first semester. There are many benefits to securing a paraprofessional position on campus. You can learn many skills in these roles—skills that are valued by employers, such as teamwork, conflict resolution, interpersonal skills. Often employment in one area leads to other opportunities on campus. Paraprofessional students are often seen as student leaders on campus. You have close contact with staff who often serve as mentors and references for other opportunities. When you serve in a paraprofessional position you typically get to know the campus well and are "in the know" about various opportunities and events. And you get paid!

VOICES FROM CAMPUS 6.1

Jessica

I made it through my first year of college okay. It was a struggle to finance everything but we got through it as a family. In my second semester, all students got an email about paraprofessional jobs. I didn't really know what those were. I mean it sounded like semi-professional jobs, right? I talked to a few upperclassmen and it turns out that a lot of the leadership roles like orientation leader, resident assistant/advisor, peer mentor, student union assistant, and even the recreation and wellness staff are paid positions.

There was a pretty tough process to apply for these, and I had to go to an information session to learn about all of them. I participated in a group interview for some of them as well. My grades and involvement in my first year also played a role in getting a position. I'm happy that I got above a 3.0 and joined the dance team in my first year because I'm pretty sure it helped me land a job as a resident assistant/advisor. As an R.A. the cost of my room has been reduced, and I get a single-occupancy room all to myself. I will also get a monthly stipend. I will need to be trained and then have hours I will need to stay in the building and be on duty. I also need to provide support and programs for the residents on my floor. I'm really excited and think the position will help me in my long-term career goal of teaching high school students.

My family is so happy because it will make this year much more affordable. Like any job, I need to be responsible and manage the R.A. role, classes, and course/class work but I'm willing to do it, especially if it helps my family.

YOUR TURN 6.2

Campus Resources

Below is the beginning of a list of campus offices and departments that typically hire students. You can use the list to start your job search process. Find the office/department on the campus website and fill in the contact information and location. There are empty rows for you to fill in other opportunities you find in your exploration.

Office or Department	Location	Contact Person
Residence Life		
Dining Services		
Catering Services		
Student Union		
Wellness Center		
Admissions Office		
Multicultural Center		
Library		
New Student Programs		
Leadership and Involvement		
Campus Recreation		
Post Office		
Service Learning Office		
Student Activities		
Tutoring Center		

6.3: Finding a Job off Campus

You may have additional opportunities for employment off campus where you can earn income. You can even explore these opportunities on the Internet before you arrive on campus. There may be local businesses that hire students to do everything from delivering pizza to managing a retail store. Explore what businesses are in your college or university community. If you can apply online before the fall semester begins, do so.

Can You Walk to Work?

If you do not have a vehicle, your off-campus job must be located close to campus. Many campus communities have local businesses that are a short walk from campus. Why? Because they know many students will come to campus without a car and they will need to shop, dine, and buy personal care items. Applying to these businesses prior to the start of the semester will give you an advantage in landing a job before all your classmates come to campus.

What Can You Do "After Hours"?

You are going to be occupied during the day with classes. Finding employment in the late afternoon, early evening, and on the weekend can add income without taking away time from your academic schedule. Many faculty and staff will hire students they know to provide childcare or tutoring for their children. These opportunities are a great source of income and give you the ability to earn money with flexibility.

You can also apply online to websites that prescreen childcare providers, in-home caregivers, and tutors for families in a local community. These sites often require a background check as a part of the process to recommend you to families. Tasks might include babysitting, running errands for an older adult, or helping a student prepare schoolwork.

Already Have a Job in High School?

Great! If you work for a national company or chain, find out if they offer the opportunity for employees to transfer to a new location. You may find that your high school job can move to wherever you are going to school. You can inquire about this policy in the human resources department of your current job. The company may also allow you to transfer back and forth between the two locations during breaks or holidays. This flexibility will allow you to work year-round and provide a job during college that you already know how to do.

VOICES FROM CAMPUS 6.2

Adam

I finally chose where I am going to college. My family is helping me pay tuition, room, and for my meal plan. I know I am lucky. My parents talked to me last week and told me that any out-of-pocket expenses are my responsibility. I get it … if I want to buy something or go out to eat I need to find a job.

As a high school student, I started working three years ago at a national discount store in my town. I like the work and my boss has been pretty happy with my performance. I know the discount store procedures for most spots in the store from stocking shelves to the cash register. When I met with my boss to tell her that I was going away to college she asked me where I was going. She pulled up the store locator and sure enough there is a branch of the store that is really close to campus. She told me I could request an internal transfer and if there was a position at that store they would hire me. I'm psyched! I can start as soon as my first-year orientation is over, and I can transfer back and forth during breaks. When I am at school I will work at that store, and when I come home for my breaks I can work at my hometown store.

My parents are happy that my boss helped me navigate this process. I did not know that national chains do transfers all the time but it makes sense. I'm already trained and can start without any additional work on the store manager's part. Bonus … I get the store discount for swag for my room!

Have Car, Will Travel?

There will always be jobs in a college community. If you have transportation, then you will be able to look for a job that is a little farther from campus. Depending on where you want to work or where you have experience, check out the local mall and apply online over the summer. Many students work in restaurants during college as waitstaff or in food delivery positions.

Other students find jobs at home improvement stores that offer seasonal work in lawn and garden, holiday, and other departments. Where you find a job will be up to you, but the earlier you start the better.

6.4: Home for the Holidays?

One of the great benefits of the college semester system is that there is typically a 4–6-week winter break. The break generally happens from mid-December to mid-January. This time frame is the same time almost all retailers are hiring seasonal help. Seasonal employment is intended to be short term in nature and is often more hours per week than is typical for retail work. Seasonal employment is a wonderful way to earn money while you are on break without making a long-term commitment. You will probably work a lot of hours, but all those hours translate to all that pay!

If you do not want to work a traditional retail position, you can consider some other types of employment—selling Christmas trees and other seasonal items, shoveling snow, cutting lawns, house sitting, pet sitting, etc. are all ways to gain extra cash.

Whatever employment you can find over the holiday break will help you financially in the following semester. Remember, you will return to campus and must buy or rent a whole new set of textbooks. The trick to landing these jobs is to apply before or during the Thanksgiving break. When applying, have your final exam schedule with you so you know exactly when you are available to be hired for a seasonal job. Once you find a job, confirm your start date with the human resource office and show up ready to go.

6.5: Are You Ready for the Summer?

The lazy days of summer do not really happen for most college students today. You will need to earn money and/or gain experience during the summer break. You will want to decide what jobs are available where you live and how they might enhance your experience in terms of your long-term career goals. Regardless of the jobs you apply for, you will want to begin a summer job search around the time of spring break. Spring break is a good time to get applications submitted and you may get a jump on the opportunities before other students apply! Like working during the winter break, you should have your final exam schedule with you when you apply so you can let potential employers know exactly when you can start employment. Many summer employers will also want to know if you are taking a family vacation and your last day of employment as you prepare to return to college.

Some students choose an internship over a summer job. Internships provide experience in a career path and are incredibly valuable as you will gain "real life" experience in your major. You will be in a setting that helps you learn about a business, school, or non-profit that will greatly enhance your résumé. Once you graduate, employers consider these experiences very favorably because they know you have been successful in a specific field and understand how similar types of organizations work.

What is the downside? Most internships are unpaid. You need to consider this fact when applying to internship programs. Additionally, if the internship is not in your hometown you will need to fund housing, food, and transportation to the internship site.

What is the upside? Depending on the internship site, you may be a candidate for employment post-graduation. Many an intern has worked so hard and so impressively at their internship that they were offered a job. It can and does open doors for many students.

6.6: Paid Internships

Can you have an internship and get paid? The answer is of course! There are great jobs in the summer for virtually every major a student may pursue. You just need to get creative and think broadly about summer employment. Interested in becoming a teacher? A job at a summer camp will help you gain experience working and instructing children. Want to gain business experience? Find a job at a local bank or working in the marketing department of a non-profit in your community. Are you interested in helping people as a social work or psychology major? See if a local assisted-care facility is hiring for the summer or if the local Boys & Girls Club has summer programs for young people. Majoring in pre-med or nursing? Check out the local pharmacies or community health organizations. The possibilities are endless!

6.7: The Take Away

- Most students have some type of employment during their undergraduate experience.
- Preparing to find a job is your first step in the process.
- There are many types of employment opportunities both on campus and off campus.
- Do not forget to think "outside of the box" to gain experience and compensation.

UNIT III: FINANCES AND YOUR FUTURE

THE COSTS OF GRADUATION

Trevor

Graduation was awesome! I know my mom is so proud of me! It feels great but also weird. I've spent four years living on campus and now I am moving back home to continue my job search. I got a lot of help from the career center on campus. And I've had a few interviews but no offers yet. I am applying for jobs and sending out my cover letter and résumé to human resource departments in companies that are a good match for my degree in marketing.

There is a lot of pressure because my student loan repayments begin in six months. Once I get a job, I'm going to live with my mom for a year to save money for my first apartment and all the expenses of moving. Long term, I want my MBA so I may be asking about tuition benefits when I get a job offer. I guess I'm an adult now!

You may not be ready to read this chapter. You may not have even started your first year, but your time in college will go quickly and you will want to be prepared. You may not read it right now, but once you finish your first year of college, you will want to come back to this chapter so you can begin to set goals for the future and think about your finances post-graduation and beyond.

This chapter will help you understand more about the repayment of loans and other expenses after graduation including finding your own place to live and the costs associated with a professional job search. In Chapter 8, you can learn about the financial decisions required as you think about pursuing graduate or professional school.

7.1: Living With Loans

Throughout this book, we have discussed the benefits and costs of assuming student loans. Now that you have graduated, the loans will quickly become due! Your collective amount of debt may seem overwhelming, even if you kept track and were vigilant about the total sum. Besides a mortgage, student loan debt may be the largest single debt in your life.

It is important to remember that your student loan repayment will impact your credit score and history for a lifetime. Whenever you apply for a credit card, car loan, mortgage, or even to rent an apartment your credit score will be considered. Why does this matter? Because the higher your credit score the easier it is to borrow money and finance purchases. Sometimes a high credit score may offer you lower interest rates when borrowing money or will allow a security deposit to be waived. Student loan repayment generally begins six months after you graduate. This short time period gives you time to find a job and begin budgeting to meet your expenses. If you are going on to graduate/professional school, some of your loans may be deferred until you complete your next degree; others may require you to pay the interest immediately.

If you do not know how much student debt you have accumulated, you can access the National Student Loan Data System (NSLDS) at www.nslds.ed.gov to view your guaranteed loans. To find out your private student loans you can go to www.creditreport.com to look up your private lenders or check with your financial aid office. Once you understand your total debt burden, you may consider consolidating all your federal student loan debt into one or two loans to reduce your monthly interest rate. Private loans must be dealt with separately.

Once you get a full-time job, you need to create a monthly list of your expenses including student loan debt. You want to prioritize repayment, even though it may impact other areas of your decision making. For example, you may not want to share an apartment with a roommate but doing so will help reduce your living expenses and allow you stay on track with student loan repayment. There are also repayment programs that factor in your income to determine a reasonable repayment amount per year. As your annual salary increases, so will the amount you repay. This information can be found at www.studentaid.gov, and you can apply for these plans at www.studentloans.gov. This graduated repayment plan may help you in the early years of your employment and professional career. Remember, as you gain professional experience your salary will hopefully grow. So it is possible that a few years after graduation this debt should become less of a burden.

During the span of repayment, you may have challenges. You may lose a job or have long-term medical issues. It will be important for you to communicate any life changes to all your student loan providers/lenders. If you have a challenge in your life, most student loan providers will require documentation from you in order to defer your loans, even for a short time. You may not think the change is significant but from the perspective of the lender, it may be enough to defer your loans in the short or long term. Whether you have a job loss, wedding, name change, or a new address, you want to stay in touch with your lenders to ensure you stay on top of your repayment. Please note: Student loans may or may not be forgiven even when declaring bankruptcy.

7.2: Spend Money to Make Money? YES!

Searching for your first professional job can be exciting but expensive! In a previous chapter, we discussed the importance of finding the best attire for your job search. It may be time to figure out a new interview outfit. You do not have to spend a lot of money but you may want to invest in some new clothes as you move on to this next step. Whether you will be interviewing for a job or graduate/professional school you will want to make sure you are appropriately dressed for the situation.

If you are invited for an on-site interview, you will need to travel to the location. If the location is within driving distance, travel may not be a financial burden. Other opportunities may require you to travel by plane or train to the interview and perhaps stay the night in a hotel. When an employer asks you to travel for an interview they may cover your expenses. Some potential employers will arrange for your travel and others may have you plan your own travel and reimburse you following the interview. You will need to keep receipts and complete paperwork as requested. It is appropriate to ask an employer if they will reimburse travel expenses. If they do not, you will need to determine if the expense is worth the opportunity for you. If there is a possibility that you can land your dream job, you may want to take on the expense.

Once you are offered a job, you may need to relocate to a new city, state, or even another country. The farther you go from your home, the more expensive the relocation cost. Packing up your belongings and renting a truck may not be a big expense. Shipping everything to a new state and getting yourself there can financially add up. Anytime you move, you will want to evaluate your belongings. The less you move, the lower the cost. You may be able to leave your cherished childhood mementos or climate-dependent clothes and equipment at home! Some employers assist new employees with moving expenses. You can ask if they offer this benefit when you are offered the position!

7.3: Go Home or Go Roam?

Now that you are a college graduate you will need to find a place to live. If you found a job near your family home, you may want to consider living there for a short time. Not everyone wants to live in their family home after graduation, but there are good financial reasons for living at home that may help you in the long term.

The cost of living independently can be much more than you might imagine. Rent, utilities, and Internet can vary from city to city. Most first-time renters will need to supply a month's rent and a security deposit which may equal an additional month's rent. You may need to pay a security deposit for your utilities and Internet service too. Following graduation, you may not have that kind of cash on hand. Living in your family home, even for a few months, could help you save for these expenses.

If you do decide to live in your family home, you will need to have an honest conversation with your family about their expectations. Make sure to ask your family first and do not assume that you can live there for free! Will you contribute to the family expenses each month? Will your family expect you to help around the house? If so, what might be your responsibilities besides taking care of yourself? Remember, just because you are a college graduate does not mean the people you live with won't have some expectations of you, even if you are working full time.

If you have relocated for your job or graduate/professional school, finding a place to rent can be challenging and exciting! You can re-search rental properties online and then make appointments to see various spaces. Of course, this process can only happen if where you are relocating is within a reasonable drive from home and you have time to do the research prior to starting your new job or graduate/professional school. There is no better way to get a sense of your new community than visiting it as you search for housing.

It is important to ask the right questions about renting. What is included in the rent? At some properties, all expenses are included. Typical expenses are utilities, cable, Internet, garbage removal, lawn care, and parking. At other rental properties, no expenses are included which means you will need to pay for these expenses and the rent. You will need to set up appointments to have your cable and utilities activated and often there is a fee associated with this activation. Many newer properties have amenities such as a pool, a community center, or a fitness center which may or may not be included with the rent. These amenities can help you reduce expenses you might incur with a gym membership. You will want to factor this information into your decision making.

If you cannot travel to visit properties, make a phone appointment to discuss the properties with the rental agency. You want to know everything about the rental property prior to signing a lease. You may want to consider signing a short-term lease in case you find a better location or property once you have relocated. You might even find some co-workers who want to share a living space.

Most rental properties will perform a credit check prior to issuing you a lease. Some may also ask for references. The lease is a legally binding document, and your landlord will want to be sure you can pay the rent each month. Your credit history is impacted by late payments on credit cards, student loans, and vehicle loans. If you have not started your job, the rental company may want your employer to verify your employment through the human resources department.

Some graduates are averse to renting and want to buy a home, condo, or apartment. To purchase property, you will need to have a down payment in cash and apply for a mortgage. Qualifying for a mortgage requires financial documentation. You will be asked to supply documentation of your salary. It might take you a few months of full-time employment to qualify for mortgage financing. If you want to purchase a home, you need to be conscious of your credit score. This score is adversely impacted by late payments to your student loans, credit cards, and vehicle payments. You want to have the highest possible credit score to help you get the best interest rate on your mortgage. Buying a property is a big step but often a great long-term decision in building for your future.

Check out Your Turn 7.1 below to navigate expenses to living inde-pendently. Use the worksheet to determine the cost of your living options by listing the rent and other expenses. Then, make sure to include some thinking about the amenities that may be offered for each option. The worksheet will give you a realistic sense of your monthly living expenses minus transportation, food, clothing, and—do not forget—student loans.

YOUR TURN 7.1

Weighing the Cost of Independent Living

Expenses	Option A Cost	Option B Cost	Option C Cost	Amenities	Option A Amenities	Option B Amenities	Option C Amenities
Monthly Rent				Gym			
Security Deposit				Pool			
Utilities (heat, water, electric, gas)				Included?			
Internet				Included?			
Cable				Included?			
Garbage Removal				Included?			
Parking Fee				Included?			
Condo/ Apartment Association Fee and/or Pet Fee				None?			
Renters Insurance (check with your insurance provider)				N/A			
Other							
TOTAL COST				**AMENITIES RATING**			

VOICES FROM CAMPUS 7.2

Xander

I am so excited about graduating! I have a job and am ready to begin my adult life. There still is a lot to consider in terms of finances. While I really want my own apartment after living four years with all types of roommates, I also want to be smart about my next steps. My annual salary is okay, but I will need to stay on budget to cover all of the new expenses I will have now. I have a car payment, car insurance, rent, utilities, and food. And I want to have a social life! I also really want to start a small savings plan. I need to have money saved in case an unexpected expense like a car repair comes up.

7.4: The Take Away

- There are many financial realities when you graduate from college and move into employment and/or graduate/professional education.

- Loan repayment is essential to maintain a healthy financial future.

- Establishing a realistic monthly budget is important and is good practice regardless of your income.

- Most opportunities come with a cost. Weighing the benefits and costs, reflecting on the information, and making an informed decision are important to your success.

HERE WE GO AGAIN! GRADUATE AND PROFESSIONAL SCHOOL

Many college graduates choose to pursue a graduate or professional degree. And many professions require a post-graduate degree. For example, if you want to be a lawyer or a medical doctor or a veterinarian, you will need to have an advanced degree. If you want to pursue an academic career as a professor or researcher, you will need to pursue graduate education. Many other professions require a degree in addition to your bachelor's degree. Some students want to continue their education and learn more about a new field or discipline.

As you begin to think about graduate or professional school you want make sure you do a lot of research. Graduate and professional school is a big investment. It is important to talk to faculty members in your field of interest. They will be a great source of information about graduate programs in the field. They most likely have colleagues at other institutions that you can contact for more information. The career center at your institution will be a valuable resource. The staff will help you understand how to research graduate programs and how to begin the application process. Additionally, you can do your own research on the Internet by navigating to the graduate programs on their website.

8.1: Now or Later??

Some students elect to enroll in graduate or professional education immediately following their undergraduate experience. For some programs, it is best to go directly from your undergraduate experience to your graduate experience. For example, most students pursuing a medical degree go directly following undergraduate graduation.

Students may choose to begin their employment first and then pursue an advanced degree. Many times, having employment experience enhances both your application and experience in graduate school. Regardless of when you choose to attend, there are associated costs.

VOICES FROM CAMPUS 8.1

Noel

Many of my college friends are graduating and getting jobs. They are making money, moving out of their family homes, and starting their adult lives. I really want a job too, but my career goal is to become a physician's assistant which requires a graduate degree.

The programs are tough to get into, but I got into a great graduate program and I start a week after graduation. My advisor from my college told me I need to be prepared to work even harder than I did as an undergraduate. I'm excited but nervous. I'm taking on more student loans to pay for graduate school. I need to be successful so I can land a job as a physician's assistant and begin repaying what I owe.

8.2: Applications, Tests, Interviews ... Oh, My!

Like your preparation for your undergraduate experience, you will need to plan for the costs associated with applying to graduate school. The application costs to apply to graduate and professional schools are often higher than an undergraduate application fee. You may be able to have the fee waived, but you will need to contact the graduate studies office to inquire about the possibility.

Additionally, there are often standardized tests that are required of applicants. The costs of these standardized tests differ depending on which test you need to take as part of your application. You want to look carefully at each application process to understand which standardized tests, if any, are required.

As part of your application to graduate school, you will need to provide your undergraduate transcripts. There is often a cost associated with having your transcripts sent to your prospective institution(s). Even if you pursue graduate education at your undergraduate institution, there may be a cost for transferring your transcripts!

An interview is frequently part of the application and assistantship/fellowship (more about that later) process. Although technology may be used in cases where distance is an issue, many institutions will want to have a face-to-face interview with you. Sometimes these interviews are done at professional conferences, which is a bonus if you have already budgeted to attend the conference. You will want to think about the cost of travel and accommodations to the one or more schools to which you apply.

8.3: Graduate School Financing

Once you have been accepted to graduate or professional school and you decide about which offer you will take, you will have to, once again, revisit the financing process. As a graduate student, you can complete a FAFSA application. You may be eligible for loans. Just as you have done throughout your undergraduate career, you will want to think carefully about taking loans to finance this advanced degree. The loans you take will be added to the loans you have already assumed. You will need to familiarize yourself with which loans (both undergraduate and graduate) require interest payment immediately and which loans can be deferred until your degree completion. It is important to understand that the types of funds available to graduate students differ from the funds available to you as an undergraduate.

8.4: The Good News!

There is some good news about financing your graduate education. Many graduate and professional schools offer assistantships and fellowships to graduate students. Assistantships and fellowships differ from institution to institution. Typically, these opportunities provide tuition remission (they pay your tuition) and a stipend in exchange for work, teaching, and/or research. These experiences and compensation are determined by the institution, and it is best to consult the institution's website, office of graduate studies, and/or the faculty in the department.

Each program you pursue may have a unique way of offering students funding. Some may offer you a fellowship or assistantship as part of your acceptance package. Many will direct you to opportunities on campus or match you with departments who have funding opportunities. Some programs may discourage you from working or even pursuing a funding opportunity.

Another way to finance graduate and professional education is through your employer. You may decide to begin employment before pursuing graduate education. Your employer may provide professional development and/or continued education benefits. This compensation for course/class work is a bonus to your benefit package! When considering a job offer you may want to ask about these types of benefits. Additionally, if you are employed by a government or not-for-profit organization you may be eligible for loan forgiveness through the Public Loan Forgiveness Program. You can find out additional information about this program at https://studentaid.ed.gov/sa/repay-loans/forgiveness-cancellation/public-service.

Working full time (or even part time) and attending graduate school can seem daunting. It is a big commitment but it can be done. Many graduate programs offer classes in the late afternoon, evening, and during the summer months, making it more convenient for students who are employed during the day. As you explore various programs, make sure that you understand whether the program can be completed part time!

VOICES FROM CAMPUS 8.2

Xander

And just like that, I am a student all over again! I am excited to start graduate school at a new university. I found out I was accepted in fall of my senior year of my undergraduate experience. I started seeking financial assistance as soon as I got in. I applied for everything I could—graduate assistantships, teaching fellowships, and as a research assistant in a lab. I got a half-time graduate assistantship that will really help with the cost. Graduate school, for me, will be two years, so I just need to keep working hard to get to my goal.

8.5: The Take Away

- Graduate and professional school is often the next step in one's education but it often comes with significant costs.
- There are ways to finance graduate and professional school that are different than how you thought about financing your undergraduate degree.
- Employers may be willing to help finance your graduate degree.

8.6: Wrapping It Up

Whew, who knew there was so much to know and learn about financing one's education? It is complicated and expensive! As you have learned throughout this book, it is important to do your research before making any financial decisions. You want to carefully weigh the benefits and costs of all financial decisions as most financial decisions impact you far into your future. Make sure to carefully think about the benefit of taking loans and pursuing graduate or professional education and weigh those benefits against the return. Does the potential result outweigh the cost of increased debt? Your thoughtful research and reflection will help you answer this question!

Good luck!!

REFERENCES

Astin, A. (1999). Student involvement: A developmental theory for higher education. *Journal of College Student Development, 40*(5), 518–529.

Baxter-Magolda, M. (2002). Helping students make their way to adulthood: Good company for the journey. *About Campus, 6*(6), 2–9.

Carnevale, A. P., Smith, N., Melton, M., & Price, E. (2015). *Learning while earning: The new normal.* Georgetown University: Center on Education and the Workforce.
Federal Student Aid. (2017). www.studentaid.ed.gov/

Gallup-Purdue Index. (2014). *Great jobs, great lives.* Washington, DC: Gallup.

National Center for Educational Statistics. (2017). https://nced.ed.gov/
—The National Postsecondary Student Aid Study. Retrieved from https://nces. ed.gov/surveys/npsas/index.asp.

Schriener, L. (2010). The "thriving quotient": A new vision for student success. *About Campus, 15*(2), 2–10.

APPENDIX

WHERE TO TURN— ADDITIONAL RESOURCES

A Timeline for Financing Your College Education

Time Frame	Tasks
Spring of High School Junior Year	✔ Explore college and university options ✔ Begin campus visits
Senior Year	
August/September	✔ Develop list of colleges and universities to which you wish to apply ✔ Identify application process/cost for each institution ✔ Explore tuition and other fees for each institution
October	✔ College essays written and proofread ✔ Request recommendations from teachers, counselors, etc. ✔ Complete the FAFSA
November	✔ Apply for admission ✔ Begin to investigate scholarships through community agencies and other avenues
January/February	✔ Files taxes as soon as possible! ✔ Begin evaluating admission offers as they arrive
March/April	✔ Attend on-campus events such as Accepted Student Days, other invited events
April	✔ Evaluate all admissions offers from each institution ✔ Evaluate each offer along with the financial aid award; rank order

Time Frame	Tasks
May 1st	✔ Pay your admissions deposit to your chosen institution ✔ Pay any other deposits and fees necessary to hold your place in the class
Summer	✔ Explore private loans ✔ Meet with lenders ✔ Follow up on scholarships ✔ Work, work, work ✔ Save, save, save
Each Year Going Forward	✔ Complete FAFSA by October ✔ File your taxes ASAP ✔ Apply for on-campus and off-campus employment ✔ Keep track of your loans and repayment schedule ✔ Save, save, save

In Print

Chany, K. (2016). *Paying for college without going broke.* New York, NY: The Princeton Review. (ISBN: 978-1101920435)
An annually updated financial aid guide detailing the FAFSA application process.

Hamel, A. V., & Furlong, J. S. (2012). *The graduate school funding handbook.* Philadelphia, PA: University of Pennsylvania Press. (ISBN: 978-0812207071)
This book provides information on graduate school tuition, fellowships, work-study opportunities, and other types of funding available for graduate students.

Stack, C., & Vedvik, R. (2017). *The financial aid handbook: Getting the education you want for the price you can afford.* Wayne, NJ: Career Press. (ISBN: 978-1632650825)
A detailed manual about the financial aid application and payment process.

Tanabe, G., & Tanabe, K. (2017). *The ultimate scholarship book 2018: Billions of dollars in scholarships, grants and prizes.* Belmont, CA: SuperCollege. (ISBN: 978-1617601224)
A detailed book of information on scholarships, eligibility, and the scholarship application process.

The College Board. (2017). *Scholarship handbook 2018.* New York, NY: College Board (ISBN: 978-1457309274)
A book used to keep track of scholarship applications and find appropriate scholarship programs.

Hurley, J. F. (2015). *The best way to save for college: A complete guide to 529 plans.* Pittsford, NY: Savingforcollege.com Publications. (ISBN: 978-0981549149)
This book provides a guide to saving strategies for college.

Ragins, M. (2013). *Winning scholarships for college: An insider's guide.* New York, NY: Holt Paperbacks. (ISBN: 978-0805099478)
A guide to finding the best scholarships, when and how to apply for them, and what to include on your application.

Peterson's. (2017). *How to get money for college 2018.* Albany, NY: Peterson's. (ISBN:978-0768941586)
A fully updated overview of financial aid percentages, changes to the FAFSA application, and financial aid tips.

Peterson's. (2017). *Four-year colleges 2018.* Albany, NY: Peterson's. (ISBN: 978-0768941234)
This book compares costs of four-year colleges, provides scholarship guidance, and assistance for financial aid.

On the Web

Paying For College

https://bigfuture.collegeboard.org/pay-for-college
A link to the College Board website explaining how to apply for financial aid and scholarships.

My Scholly

https://myscholly.com/
A scholarship search engine that provides a personalized list of the most applicable scholarships for each student.

Top 10 Tips for Saving Money in College

https://www.youtube.com/watch?v=xY3k_abmOQ0
A link to a video explaining 10 ways you can save money while in college.

How to Fill Out the FAFSA

https://www.youtube.com/watch?v=LK0bbu0y5AM
A guided video to filling out the FAFSA application.

Common FAFSA Mistakes

https://www.youtube.com/watch?v=AIARWTi3Y5E

A live stream video chat from U.S. News Education about the most common mistakes students and parents make on the FAFSA application.

9 High-Paying Part-Time Jobs for College Students

http://www.businessinsider.com/high-paying-part-time-jobs-2015-10/#non-profit-charity-

A list of part-time jobs with high wages suitable for college students.

Budgeting 101

http://www.bestcolleges.com/resources/budgeting-in-college/

Quick read on how to create a budget for college expenses.

Scholarship Finder

https://www.careeronestop.org/toolkit/training/find-scholarships.aspx

Provides a list of scholarships based specifically on each student's needs.

Federal Work-Study

https://www2.ed.gov/programs/fws/index.html

Description of the work-study program for FAFSA eligible students.

5 Apps for Setting a College Student Budget

http://www.rasmussen.edu/student-life/blogs/college-life/awesome-college-student- budget-apps/

A list of phone apps that are helpful in creating and maintaining a college budget.

The College Grant Database

http://www.collegegrant.net/

Gives detailed description of a variety of federal grants and links to apply to them.

Scholarship Essay Writing Tips

https://www.internationalstudent.com/essay_writing/scholarship_essay/
Step-by-step guidance to writing a strong scholarship essay.

Fellowships for Graduate Students

https://www.gradschools.com/financial-aid/graduate-fellowships-scholarships/
fellowships-for-graduate-students
Directory for graduate students with information regarding fellowship opportunities.

Learn to Manage Your Time in College

https://www.usnews.com/education/blogs/the-college-experience/2011/10/05/
learn-to-manage-your-time-in-college
Link to article with advice on how to split your time wisely.

Graduate School Search

https://www.gradschools.com/
Compares graduate schools to find the most compatible school for each student.

Budgeting Tips

https://studentaid.ed.gov/sa/prepare-for-college/budgeting/budgeting-tips
Tips for college students on how to budget money.

On Campus

Student Financial Aid

Assists students in applying for and obtaining financial aid and scholarships.

Student Financial Services

Provides students with information about tuition, billing, financial aid, and scholarships.

Office of the Bursar

Office that generates your bill and where you go to pay your bill.

Registrar's Office

Provides administrative academic support for current and former students. Questions about registration, transfer credits, grades, etc. can be answered by the staff in this office.

Orientation or New Student Programs

Introduces students to opportunities on campus and aids in the transition into college life.

Division of Student Affairs

Provides support and opportunities to students as they navigate their lives on campus. A good place to start with any questions about college life!

Residence Life

Provides students with information about living on campus.

Career Development Center

Provides career development services such as résumé development, interview preparation, job search strategies. This office may also provide a list of employment opportunities for students.

Student Union

Often the "hub" on campus. Often provides programming, dining services, bookstore, meeting spaces, student organization offices, events.

Counseling Center

Provides emotional and psychology support services for students.

Student Employment Center

On some campuses, this center is a source for finding on-campus jobs.

Writing Center

Assists students with their writing skills.

Tutoring and Supplemental Instruction

Supports students, often through peer tutoring, with course/class work that may be challenging.

Alumni Association

Provides scholarships, mentors, and awards for students from alumni members.

Human Resources

Support services for people seeking employment and opportunities for professional development. They may provide a list of employment opportunities for students.

Graduate Studies Office

The best place to start with questions about applying for graduate school and for understanding how graduate assistantship and fellowships work.

University Libraries

Source of textbooks, print resources, computers, and study rooms. University libraries are staffed with reference librarians who can help you find resources.

In the Community

Local Library

Source for print resources.

Religious Organizations

Provide potential job listings or scholarships.

Boys & Girls Club

Provides advice, guidance, and resources for the future. May have scholarship opportunities.

Girl Scouts

http://www.girlscouts.org/en/our-program/scholarships.html
Leadership development organization for girls.

Boy Scouts

http://www.scouting.org/home/boyscouts/youth/scholarships.aspx
Leadership development organization for boys.

Local Jaycees Branch

Leadership organization encouraging young people to help the community.

YMCA and YWCA

Organizations for youth development and social change.
*Local scholarships available.

Kiwanis

http://www2.kiwanis.org/childrensfund/impact-and-programs/scholarship-opportunities#
Organization encouraging social change through younger generations of students.

4-H

http://4-h.org/parents/4-h-youth-in-action/
Enhances youth leadership skills through various science, health, agriculture, and citizenship projects.

Rotary Clubs

https://www.rotary.org/en/our-programs/scholarships

Joins local people together to do service projects for their community.

Youth Service America

http://ysa.org/awards/

Provides guidance to young people through community service, philanthropy, and advocacy.

Big Brothers/Big Sisters of America

Partners children and adult volunteers to create a meaningful relationship that will give the child personal support.

* Local scholarships available.

Key Club

http://www.keyclub.org/contestsawards.aspx

Performs local community service acts and encourages leadership skills.

The First Tee

https://thefirsttee.org/programs/youth-opportunities/first-tee-scholars-program/

Youth development organization that instills values, morals, and leadership through the game of golf.

Girls Inc.

http://www.girlsinc.org/about/national-scholars.html

Program designed to empower young girls to break down social barriers through community service.

Junior Achievement

https://www.juniorachievement.org/web/ja-usa/scholarship-info

An organization surrounding the professional and educational development of youth.

CPSIA information can be obtained
at www.ICGtesting.com
Printed in the USA
LVHW080632280722
724570LV00005B/18